Kitchen Cures

JJ DeSpain

Linnea Lundgren

Michele Price Mann

Publications International, Ltd.

JJ DeSpain writes about health, consumerism, and senior issues for national magazines in the United States and Canada. A former critical-care nurse, she is a college instructor, coauthor of *Government Secrets* and author of *Life-Saving Health Secrets, Inside Info,* and *Money Secrets.*

Linnea Lundgren has ten years experience researching, writing, and editing for newspapers and magazines. She is the author of four books including *Living Well with Allergies.*

Michele Price Mann is a freelance writer who has written for such publications as *Weight Watchers* magazine and *Southern Living* magazine. Formerly assistant health and fitness editor at *Cooking Light* magazine, her professional passion is learning and writing about health issues.

Consultant: Ara Der Marderosian, Ph.D.

Illustrator: Jeff Moores

ACKNOWLEDGMENTS:
Pages 16, 88, 89, 115, 164, 165, 176: Excerpts from *The Complete Book of Ayurvedic Home Remedies,* by Vasant Lad. Copyright © 1998 by Vasant Lad. Used by permission of Harmony Books, a division of Random House. For more information on Ayurveda visit www.ayurveda.com.

Page 33: Excerpt from *Folk Remedies from Around the World,* by John Heinerman.

Page 34: Excerpt from *Healing Power of Food,* by Amanda Ursell.

Pages 34, 90, 159: Excerpts from *Heinerman's Encyclopedia of Healing Herbs and Spices,* by John Heinerman. Copyright © 1996. Reprinted with permission of Prentice Hall Direct.

Pages 46, 47, 81: Excerpts from *The Complete Home Wellness Handbook,* by John Edward Swartzberg.

Page 58: Excerpt from *Natural Folk Remedies,* by Lelord Kordel.

Pages 73, 75, 76, 90: Excerpts from *Miracle Food Cures from the Bible,* by Reese Dubin. Copyright © 1999. Reprinted with permission of Prentice Hall Direct.

Page 131: Excerpt from the American Heart Association web site, www.americanheart.org.

Page 163: Excerpt from *Hoosier Home Remedies,* by Varro E. Tyler.

Page 177: Excerpt from *The Complete Home Healer* by Angela Smyth. Copyright © 1991 Angela Smyth. Reprinted by kind permission of The Lisa Eveleigh Literary Agency.

This book is for information purposes and is not intended to provide medical advice. Neither Publications International, Ltd., nor the authors, consultant, editors, or publisher, take responsibility for any possible consequences from any treatment, procedure, exercise, dietary modification, action, or application of medication or preparation by any person reading or following the information in this book. The publication of this book does not constitute the practice of medicine, and this book does not attempt to replace your physician or other health care provider. Before undertaking any course of treatment, the authors, editors, consultant, and publisher advise the reader to check with a physician or other health care provider.

Contents

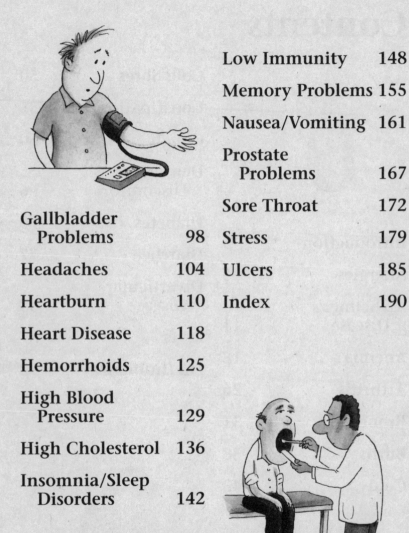

Introduction

What's cookin' in the kitchen? A lot more than you might expect. But we're not talking about meals here. What we've cooked up are hundreds of cures, treatments, and preventions for both everyday and serious health problems—all using ingredients you can find in your own kitchen.

Think of the kitchen as a personal pharmacy that you can visit in your bathrobe and slippers, 24 hours a day, 7 days a week. Open up the cupboards, peek into the refrigerator, and scan the pantry. Got baking soda? Vinegar? Tea? Milk? Honey? These are just some of the simple items that are the basis for scores of problem-solving remedies you'll find in this book—remedies that have stood the test of time as well as contemporary ones based on the latest scientific information.

Kitchen Cures covers 31 health problems, from allergies to ulcers. Each profile includes a short explanation of the causes and symptoms of the condition, followed by a host of remedies for it based on ingredients from your kitchen. The remedies are listed according to where they are typically found: the cupboard, the spice rack, the refrigerator, the sink...even the junk drawer.

So next time you or a loved one suffers from a health problem, check out the kitchen first. With *Kitchen Cures*, you'll find a whole pharmacy at your feet...er, slippers.

Allergies

BREATHING EASIER

Allergies can be called a haywire response of the immune system. Normally, the immune system guards against intruders it considers harmful to the body, such as certain viruses and bacteria. That's its job. However, in allergic people, the immune system goes a bit bonkers. It overreacts when you breathe, ingest, or touch a harmless substance. The benign culprits triggering the overreaction, such as dust, pet dander, and pollen, are called allergens.

The body's first line of defense against invaders includes the nose, mouth, eyes, lungs, and stomach. When the immune system reacts to an allergen, these body parts make great battlegrounds. Symptoms include runny nose; sneezing; watery, swollen, or red eyes; nasal congestion; wheezing; shortness of breath; a tight feeling in the chest; difficulty breathing; coughing; diarrhea; nausea; headache; fatigue; and a general feeling of misery. Symptoms can occur alone or in combination.

What Causes Allergies?

Blame your genes. The tendency to become allergic is inherited, and allergies typically develop before age 30.

What you become allergic to is based on what substances you are exposed to and how often you are exposed to them. Generally, the more you are exposed to an allergen, the more likely it is to trigger a reaction.

Unfortunately, there is no cure for allergies. But there are ways to ease your long-suffering sinuses and skin.

FROM THE CUPBOARD

BAKING SODA. One-half cup baking soda poured into a warm bath is an old New England folk remedy for soothing hives. Soak for 20 to 30 minutes.

TEA. Allergy sufferers throughout the centuries have turned to hot tea to relieve clogged-up noses and irritated mucous membranes. One of the best for symptom relief is mint tea, which has been used by the Chinese to treat allergies since the seventh century. Mint's benefits extend well beyond its

WHEN TO CALL THE DOCTOR

You can't always tell whether what's bothering you is an allergy or an infection, intolerance, or a specific disease. So check with your doctor if you experience any of these:

- Nasal problems that cause secondary symptoms, such as chronic sinus infection, or difficulty breathing
- Symptoms that last for several months
- Lack of relief from over-the-counter medications or unacceptable side effects from them
- Symptoms that interfere with your daily activities or decrease your quality of life
- Any of these warning signs of asthma: struggling to catch your breath; wheezing and coughing, especially at night or after exercise; shortness of breath; tightness in your chest

Ah-choo! God Bless You!

Pope Gregory the Great gets bragging rights on coining the phrase "God bless you" after a sneeze. During his reign in the sixth century, a plague ravaged the region. He insisted on a quick prayer as a response to the very contagious sneeze.

delicious smell. Mint's essential oils act as a decongestant, and substances within the mint contain anti-inflammatory and mild antibacterial constituents. To make mint tea: Place ½ ounce dried mint leaves in a 1-quart jar. Fill two-thirds of the jar with boiling water and steep for five minutes (inhale the steam). Let cool, strain, sweeten if desired, and drink.

From the Freezer

Ice. Wrap a washcloth around ice cubes and apply them to your sinuses for instant relief and refreshment.

From the Refrigerator

Milk. Milk does the body good, especially when it comes to hives. Wet a cloth with cold milk and lay it on the affected area for 10 to 15 minutes.

Wasabi. If you're a hay fever sufferer and sushi lover combined, this remedy will please. Wasabi, that pale green, fiery condiment served alongside California rolls, is a member of the horseradish family. Anyone who has taken too big a dollop of wasabi or plain old horseradish knows how it makes sinuses and tear ducts spring into action. That's because allyl isothiocyanate, a constituent in wasabi, promotes phlegm flow and has anti-asthmatic properties. The tastiest way to get in those allyl isothiocyanates is by slathering horseradish on your sandwich or plopping wasabi onto your favorite sushi. The last, harder-to-swallow option is to purchase grated horseradish and take ¼ teaspoon during an allergy attack.

FROM THE SPICE RACK

BASIL. To help ease an allergic reaction or hives, try dousing the skin with basil tea, a traditional Chinese folk remedy. Basil contains high amounts of an anti-allergic compound called caffeic acid. Place 1 ounce dried basil leaves into 1 quart boiling water. Cover and let cool to room temperature. Use the tea as a rinse as often as needed.

SALT. Nasal irrigation, an effective allergy-management tool that's done right at the sink every morning, uses saltwater to rid the nasal passages of mucus, bacteria, dust, and other gunk, as well as to soothe irritated passageways. All you need is 1 to 1½ cups lukewarm water (do not use softened water), a bulb (ear) syringe, ¼ to ½ teaspoon salt, and ¼ to ½ teaspoon baking soda. Mix the salt and baking soda into the water and test the temperature. To administer, suck the water into the bulb and squirt the saline solution into one nostril while holding the other closed. Lower your head over the sink and gently blow out the water. Repeat this, alternating nostrils until you've used up all the water.

Nasal irrigation isn't a pretty sight, yet it works wonders on sore noses and rids the passages of unwanted stuff.

FROM THE STOVE

STEAM. Breathing steam refreshes and soothes sore sinuses, and it helps rid the nasal passages of mucus. While it takes some time, it will make you feel wonderful! Boil several cups of water and pour into a big bowl (or a plugged sink). Place your head carefully over the bowl and drape a towel over yourself. Breathe in and out gently for 5 to 10 minutes.

When you're finished breathing steam, use the hot water for a second purpose. Let the water cool until warm, saturate a washcloth, and hold it on the sinuses (to the sides of your nose, below the eyes and above the eyebrows).

MORE DO'S AND DON'TS

- Pass up the milk. When allergies act up, skip that extra-large, whole-milk latte since dairy products thicken mucus. Try herbal tea instead.

- Shampoo before bedtime. During pollen prime time, the hair acts as one gigantic magnet, attracting flying pollen and stray mold spores. The more hair you have, and the oilier and more elaborately styled it is, the better its collection capabilities. When you lie down, these hair hitchhikers drop onto the pillow and are quickly inhaled, causing allergy symptoms that night or the next morning. To avoid being a walking collection agency, cover your hair when out for a walk or wash it before bedtime.

SPEEDY SNEEZES

Blink and you just might miss that sneeze. Sneezing, a reflex beyond your control, is caused by the irritation of nerve endings in the nose and mucous membranes. A sneeze can whip out at 100 miles per hour—quicker than you can grab a tissue to catch it. Also, your eyes naturally will close when one approaches, so yes, you will blink and miss it.

Alzheimer's Disease
ALLEVIATING SYMPTOMS

Alzheimer's disease (AD) is everyone's worst nightmare. Most diseases destroy either a physical or a mental function. Alzheimer's seizes both, slowly and steadily destroying memory, logical thought, and language. Simple tasks—how to eat or comb hair—are forgotten, and once AD sets in there's no turning back the clock.

The disease is named for Dr. Alois Alzheimer, a German doctor who, during an autopsy in 1906, discovered physical changes in the brain of a woman who had died of a strange mental illness. He found plaques and tangles in her brain, signs that are now considered hallmarks of AD.

A Progressive Disease

AD is one of a group of progressive degenerative brain disorders called dementia that affect memory, thinking, behavior, and emotion. Alzheimer's is the most common cause of dementia: Between 50 and 60 percent of all cases of dementia can be attributed to Alzheimer's.

Early symptoms include difficulty remembering names, places, or faces and trouble recalling things that just hap-

WHEN TO CALL THE DOCTOR

- When memory becomes a problem
- When normal reasoning and decision-making become difficult
- When the ability to recall simple, everyday tasks is a struggle
- When friends or family mention that there's a noticeable change in personality or memory
- When there is disorientation about time and place

pened. Personality changes and confusion when driving a car or handling money are also early symptoms. Mild forgetfulness progresses to problems in comprehension, speaking, reading, and writing. And physical breakdown occurs, too, partly because tasks such as eating and drinking are simply forgotten or too difficult to accomplish.

While we don't know the cause of AD yet, we do know there are dietary and environmental factors. A stealth virus that lies dormant for years is being studied as a possible cause. So is heredity. Aluminum has been suspected, but the jury is still out. Most researchers believe that if aluminum has a role in the development of AD, it is minor.

Although we don't have a cure for AD, the picture is not as bleak as it was a decade ago. Research is turning up remedies that can help alleviate symptoms as well as slow the advancement of the disease. Many of these can be found right in your kitchen.

FROM THE CUPBOARD

There are lots of good cures in here, not only for appetite and health but for hygiene, which can become a problem as AD progresses and personal care becomes difficult.

BAKING SODA. Since many brands of toothpaste on the market contain aluminum, perhaps try a mixture of powdered salt and baking soda. This combination makes an excellent toothpaste that can help whiten teeth and remove plaque, which contributes to cavities and gum disease. To make the mixture, pulverize salt in an electric coffee mill, or spread some on a cutting board and roll it with a pastry rolling pin, crushing it into a fine sandlike texture. Mix 1 part crushed salt with 2 parts baking soda, then dip a dampened toothbrush into the mixture and brush teeth. Rinse well, and do not swallow the mixture. Keep the powder on hand in an airtight container in your bathroom.

MEAL SUPPLEMENTS. These meal-in-a-can beverages are easy to drink, and they're fortified with vitamins and minerals.

SEEDS. Pumpkin, sesame, and sunflower seeds are packed with essential fatty acids necessary for brain function.

SESAME OIL. Depression associated with AD may be relieved with nose drops of warmed sesame oil. Use about 3 drops per nostril, twice a day. Some say you can also help relieve depression by rubbing a little of that warmed sesame oil on the top of the head and bottoms of the feet.

VINEGAR. For incontinence, clean the genital area thoroughly with equal parts vinegar and water. For a homemade deodorant (since many store-bought brands contain aluminum), combine equal amounts of water and vinegar. Dab lightly under the arms. This will not stop perspiration, but it will control odor. Cider vinegar can help relieve itchy skin. Add 8 ounces apple cider vinegar to a bathtub of warm water. Soak for at least 15 minutes.

EXERCISE EATING RESTRAINT

Recent studies indicate that the less you eat, the slower you age. "Old-age genes" may actually stop functioning when daily calories are cut back by as little as 25 percent. Some of these genes that switch off maybe linked to AD.

WHEAT GERM OR POWDERED MILK. Add to foods for extra protein.

FROM THE REFRIGERATOR

BLUEBERRIES. New evidence suggests they contain an antioxidant that may slow down age-related motor changes, such as those seen in Alzheimer's.

BOTTLED WATER. Because tap water may contain aluminum, pure bottled well or spring water may be a more brain-safe beverage. A water filter works, too. Ask your water company for an analysis of your water.

CARROTS. These are loaded with beta-carotene, which is a memory booster. Carrot and beet juice are good for the memory, too. So are okra and spinach.

CITRUS FRUITS. These fruits are loaded with vitamin C, which is believed to help protect brain nerves. Berries and some vegetables, including peppers, sweet potatoes, and green leafy vegetables, are also rich sources of vitamin C.

EGGS. It doesn't matter how you eat them. Eggs are loaded with vitamin A, which may protect brain cells and enhance brain function. Other vitamin A-rich foods include liver, spinach, milk, squash, and peaches.

FISH. Fatty acids, which AD sufferers often lack, are important in keeping those brain nerves healthy. Fish are high in fatty acids (that's why they're often called "brain food"), so it's a good idea to eat fish several times a week. Good choices include salmon, mackerel, sardines, and anchovies.

GREEN LEAFY VEGETABLES. These are high in folic acid, which may stimulate cognitive function. Other good sources of folic acid include beets, black-eyed peas and other legumes, brussels sprouts, and whole-grain foods.

ORANGE JUICE. This is another way to up your vitamin C intake, but don't combine it with buffered aspirin. The two, taken together, form aluminum citrate, which is absorbed into the body five times faster than normal aluminum.

RED VEGETABLES. Research from the Netherlands suggests that people who eat large amounts of dark red, yellow, and green vegetables may reduce their risk of dementia by 25 percent.

SOY PRODUCTS. Studies suggest that isoflavones found in soy protein may protect postmenopausal women from AD. Try these: soy milk over cereal, soy meat substitutes, tofu frozen treats. And substitute tofu for ricotta or cream cheese in recipes. Dietary guidelines suggest 20 to 25 grams soy protein per day.

FROM THE SPICE RACK

Many people with AD experience a decrease in taste, so spice up that food to tempt the taste buds and appetite. Chili powder, pepper, sage, oregano—anything that tastes good and makes food interesting will work. Don't overload on salt, though.

ALMOND EXTRACT. This contains vitamin E. Try baking some almond cookies.

CURRY. New research suggests that curcumin, an antioxidant and anti-inflammatory compound in turmeric, a spice used in yellow curry, might prevent AD. This could explain why India has one of the lowest rates of AD in the world.

GINGER. This spice can stimulate a poor appetite. Try some ginger tea or gingersnaps, or chop up some fresh ginger and mix it with a little lime juice and a pinch of salt, then chew. It will not only increase appetite but thirst, too.

LEMON OIL. Steep a few drops of lemon or peppermint oil in hot water, then inhale. These are aromatherapy stimulants; they can perk up those suffering typical AD symptoms such as lethargy or depression.

SAGE. For depression associated with AD, drink a tea made with ½ teaspoon sage and ¼ teaspoon basil steeped in 1 cup hot water twice a day.

SALT. For dry skin that occurs with age: After a shower or bath, and while the skin is still wet, sprinkle salt onto your hands and rub it all over the skin. Then rinse well. This salt massage will remove dry skin and make skin more smooth to the touch. It will also invigorate the skin and get circulation moving. Try this first thing in the morning to help you wake up. If your skin is itchy, soak in a tub of saltwater. Just add 1 cup table salt or sea salt to the bathwater. This solution will also soften skin and encourage relaxation.

TURMERIC. Curcumin, an antioxidant and anti-inflammatory compound in this spice, has been found to reduce the number of plaques in the brain of mice and thus may slow the progression of Alzheimer's. Some use this spice on its own; otherwise it is a component of curry powder.

MORE DO'S & DON'TS

- Don't serve foods with pits or bones.
- Always check food temperature. Hot and cold sensations can be numbed in people with AD, but they still can get burned.
- Don't serve foods with a mixture of textures. They may be hard to swallow.
- Serve foods that require little chewing, such as soups, ground meat, and applesauce.
- Serve several smaller meals instead of three main meals.
- Select favorite foods, especially if the appetite is poor. And keep in mind that as the disease progresses, food preferences may change.
- Play music at meals. Mealtimes can be stressful and music is relaxing. Choose songs from the patient's youth or that hold a special memory.

STATISTICS ON ALZHEIMER'S

According to statistics from the Alzheimer's Disease Education & Referral Center:

- Up to 4 million Americans have Alzheimer's.
- AD usually begins after age 60.
- AD increases with age; 3 percent of the population ages 65 to 75 have AD, and up to 50 percent of those age 85 are afflicted.
- The number of people with AD doubles every 5 years after age 65.
- Those with a sibling who has AD have a 50 percent chance of developing it.
- People who smoke more than 1 pack of cigarettes a day are 4 times more likely to develop AD as those who don't smoke.

Anemia
BUILDING YOUR BLOOD

Anemia is a condition in which your red blood cell count is so low that the blood can't carry enough oxygen to all parts of your body. Not having enough oxygen in the blood is like trying to drive a car with no oil. Your car may run for a while, but you'll soon end up with a burned-out engine. In the same way that oil nourishes your car's engine, oxygen provides needed nourishment for your body's tissues (organs, muscles, etc.), and if they aren't getting 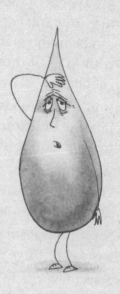 enough of that vital sustenance, you'll start feeling weak and tired. A short climb up the stairs will leave you breathless, and even a couple days of rest won't perk you up. If that describes how you feel, check with your doctor. If you do have anemia, you should take action as soon as possible. And you need to be sure you don't have a more serious condition.

Anatomy of Anemia

Your red blood cells are the delivery trucks of the body. They carry oxygen throughout your blood vessels and capillaries to feed tissues. Hemoglobin, the primary component of red blood cells, is a complex molecule and is the oxygen carrier of the red blood cell.

The body works very hard to ensure that it produces enough red blood cells to successfully carry oxygen but not too many, which can cause the blood to get too thick. Red blood cells live only 90 to 120 days. The liver and spleen get rid of the old cells, though the iron in the cells is recycled and sent back to the marrow to produce new cells.

> ### WHEN TO CALL THE DOCTOR
> * At the first sign of any of the following symptoms: weakness, unexplained fatigue, or shortness of breath. That's because anemia can mask a more serious disease.

When you're diagnosed with anemia, it usually means your red blood cell count is abnormally low, so it can't carry enough oxygen to all parts of your body, or that there is a reduction in the hemoglobin content of your red blood cells. Anemia's not a disease in itself but instead is considered a condition. However, this condition can be a symptom of a more serious illness. That's why it's always important to check with your doctor if you think you may be anemic.

The Most Common Causes of Anemia

There are many types of anemia. Some rare types are the result of a malfunction in the body, such as early destruction of red blood cells (hemolytic anemia), a hereditary structural defect of red blood cells (sickle cell anemia), or an inability to make or use hemoglobin (sideroblastic anemia). The most common forms of anemia are the result of some type of nutritional deficiency and can often be treated easily with some help from the kitchen. These common types are:

- Iron deficiency anemia. Iron deficiency anemia happens when the body doesn't have enough iron to produce hemoglobin, causing the red blood cells to shrink. And if there's not enough hemoglobin produced, the body's tissues don't get the nourishing oxygen they need. Children younger than three years of age and premenopausal women are at highest risk for developing iron deficiency anemia. Contrary to popular belief, men and older women aren't at greater risk for iron deficiency anemia. If they do end up developing the condition, it's most often the result of an ulcer.

- Vitamin B_{12} deficiency anemia. While iron deficiency anemia produces smaller than usual red blood cells, a vitamin B_{12} deficiency anemia produces oversized red blood cells. This makes it harder for the body to squeeze the red blood cells through vessels and veins. It's like trying to squeeze a marble through a straw. Vitamin B_{12}-deficient red blood cells also tend to die off more quickly than normal cells. Most people get at least the minimum amount of B_{12} that they need by eating a varied diet. If you are a vegetarian or have greatly limited your intake of meat, milk, and eggs for other health reasons, you may not get enough of the vitamin in your diet. Many older people are more at risk for vitamin B_{12} deficiency; in fact, 1 out of 100 people older than 60 years of age are diagnosed with pernicious anemia. This age group is at

IRON'S ABSORPTION EQUATION

You may not be absorbing as much iron from your foods as you think. How much you absorb is dependent on two primary factors: what kind of iron is in the food and what other nutrients the food contains. There are two types of iron, heme and non-heme. Heme, found primarily in foods of animal origin, is much more easily absorbed than non-heme iron, which is found primarily in plant products. But if you eat a vitamin C-rich food or a food rich in heme iron with your non-heme iron food, your body will take in more iron.

Here's a guide to top iron sources:

- Sources of mostly heme iron: beef liver, lean sirloin, lean ground beef, skinless chicken, pork
- Sources of non-heme iron: fortified breakfast cereal, pumpkin seeds, bran, spinach
- Sources of vitamin B_{12}: salmon (3 ounces) 2.6 mcg, beef tenderloin (3 ounces) 2.5 mcg, yogurt (1 cup) 1.4 mcg, shrimp (3 ounces) 1.3 mcg
- Sources of folic acid: spinach (½ cup) 130 mcg, navy beans (½ cup) 125 mcg, wheat germ (¼ cup) 80 mcg, avocado (½ cup) 55 mcg, orange (1 medium) 45 mcg

increased risk because they are more likely to have conditions that affect the body's ability to absorb vitamin B_{12}. Surgical removal of portions of the stomach or small intestine; atrophic gastritis, a condition that causes the stomach lining to thin; and diseases such as Crohn's can all interfere with the body's ability to absorb vitamin B_{12}. But the most common cause of vitamin B_{12} deficiency anemia is a lack of a protein called intrinsic factor. Intrinsic factor is normally secreted by the stomach; its job is to help vitamin B_{12}. Without intrinsic factor, the vitamin B_{12} that you consume in your diet just floats out as waste. In some people, a genetic defect causes the body to stop producing intrinsic factor. In other people, an autoimmune reaction, in which the body mistakenly attacks stomach cells that produce the protein, results in a lack of intrinsic factor. A vitamin B_{12} deficiency that is caused by a lack of intrinsic factor is called pernicious anemia. Pernicious anemia can be particularly dangerous because it causes neurological problems, such as difficulty walking, poor concentration, depression, memory loss, and irritability. These can usually be reversed if the condition is treated in time. Unfortunately, in the case of pernicious anemia, the stomach cannot absorb the vitamin no matter how much B_{12}-rich food you eat. So treatment requires injections of B_{12}, usually once a month, that bypass the stomach and shoot the vitamin directly into the bloodstream.

- Folic acid deficiency anemia. A deficiency of folic acid produces the same oversized red blood cells as a vitamin B_{12} deficiency. One of the most common causes of folic acid deficiency anemia is simply not getting enough in the diet. The body doesn't store up folic acid for long, so if you aren't getting enough in your diet, you will quickly become deficient. Pregnant women are most at risk for folic acid anemia because the need for folic acid increases by two-thirds during pregnancy. Adequate folic acid intake is essential from the start of pregnancy because it protects against spinal defects in the fetus.

Symptoms of Anemia

Symptoms of more severe anemia include rapid heartbeat, dizziness, headache, ringing in the ears, irritability, pale skin, restless legs syndrome, and confusion. A vitamin B_{12} or folic acid deficiency may even cause your mouth and tongue to swell. These symptoms may sound scary, but the most common forms of anemia are easily treated, especially if caught early.

Symptoms of mild to moderate anemia:

- weakness
- fatigue
- shortness of breath

Symptoms of moderate to severe anemia:

- rapid heartbeat
- dizziness
- headache
- ringing in the ears
- pale skin (especially the palms of your hands), pale or bluish fingernails
- hair loss
- restless legs syndrome
- confusion

Symptoms specific to severe vitamin B_{12} or folic acid deficiency anemia:

- swelling of the mouth or tongue

Symptoms specific to pernicious anemia:

- numbness, tingling
- depression and/or irritability
- memory loss

Because all but pernicious anemia are the result of a nutritional deficiency, the best ways to treat them can be found in the kitchen.

FROM THE CUPBOARD

BLACKSTRAP MOLASSES. Consider covering that waffle or those pancakes in a little molasses. Blackstrap molasses has long been known to be a nutritional powerhouse. Containing 3.5 mg of iron per tablespoon, blackstrap molasses has been used in folk medicine as a "blood builder" for centuries.

DRY CEREAL. Fix yourself a bowl of your favorite cereal (go for one without the sugar and the cartoon characters on the box), and you'll be waging a battle against anemia. These days many cereals are fortified with a nutrient punch of iron, vitamin B_{12}, and folic acid. Check the label for amounts per serving, pour some milk over your flakes, and dig in.

FROM THE REFRIGERATOR

BEEF LIVER. Beef liver is rich in iron and all the B vitamins (including B_{12} and folic acid). In fact, beef liver contains more iron per serving—5.8 mg per 3 ounces—than any other food. Other animal sources of iron include eggs, cheese, fish, lean sirloin, lean ground beef, and chicken.

BEETS. Beets are rich in folic acid, as well as many other nutrients, such as fiber and potassium. The best way to prepare beets is to nuke 'em in the microwave. Keep the skin on when cooking, but peel before eating. The most nutrient-dense part of the beet is right under the skin.

SPINACH. Green leafy vegetables contain loads of iron and folic acid. We're talking dark and green, so choose your leaves carefully. Iceberg lettuce is mostly water and is of little nutritive value. Spinach, on the other hand, has 3.2 mg of iron and 130 mcg of folic acid per ½ cup.

MORE DO'S AND DON'TS

- If you're a vegetarian or have cut way down on your intake of meats, milk, and eggs, be sure that you're getting adequate amounts of iron and vitamin B_{12} in your diet. With such a diet, you are at greater risk for nutritional deficiency anemias because iron from plant sources isn't absorbed as well as iron from animal sources and because vitamin B_{12} is found almost exclusively in animal foods.

- Eat foods rich in vitamin C at the same time that you eat whole grains, spinach, and legumes, in order to increase absorption of the iron they contain.

- If you drink coffee or tea, do so between meals rather than with meals, because the caffeine in these beverages reduces iron absorption.

Arthritis
PROTECTING YOUR JOINTS

Arthritis means inflamma-
tion of the joints. To the millions of Americans afflicted
by one of the 100 varieties of
arthritis, every day can be
painful. The two most preva-
lent forms of arthritis are
osteoarthritis and rheumatoid
arthritis.

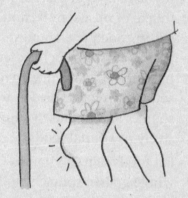

Osteoarthritis (OA), the most common form, is the
result of joint cartilage wearing down over time. When
this durable, elastic tissue is gone, bones rub directly
against one another. This causes stiffness and dull pain in
the weight-bearing joints (hips, knees, and spine) and in
the hands. The elderly are most susceptible to OA, but
athletes and those in jobs requiring repetitive movements
are also very vulnerable.

Rheumatoid arthritis (RA) is the inflammation of the
joint lining. The cause is unknown, but it is thought that
the symptoms are the result of the body turning against
itself. Symptoms of RA vary from individual to individual.
In its mildest form, it causes minor joint discomfort. More
often, however, the inflammation causes painful, stiff,
swollen joints, and in prolonged cases, severe joint damage. Unlike OA, whose symptoms are joint-specific, RA

tends to cause body-wide symptoms such as fatigue, fever, and weight loss.

While it's typically thought that old age puts one at risk for arthritis, this isn't the case with RA. RA usually develops between the ages of 20 and 50 and is more common in women than in men.

Waking up with a stiff back or swollen finger joint doesn't necessarily indicate arthritis; however, should pain, stiffness, or swelling last more than two weeks, you may have arthritis. Other symptoms include:

• Swelling in one or more joints

• Early morning stiffness

• Recurring pain or tenderness in a joint

• Inability to move a joint in a normal fashion

• Redness or warmth in a joint

• Unexplained weight loss, fever, or weakness accompanied by joint pain

There is no cure for arthritis, but many kitchen-crafted remedies can help ease the pain.

FROM THE CUPBOARD

ASPARTAME. Drink to pain relief with a sugar-free soda pop. A research experiment published in the scientific journal *Clinical Pharmacology and Therapeutics* noted that aspartame—an artificial sweetener found in brands Equal and NutraSweet—provides relief that's comparable to anti-inflammatory agents. Ask your doctor about the study and exactly how much you should drink.

EPSOM SALTS. Magnesium sulfate, otherwise known as Epsom salts, is commonly used to relieve aching joints

WHEN TO CALL THE DOCTOR

- When stiffness and pain last more than a few weeks
- If joint pain is accompanied by unexplained weight loss, fever, or weakness
- If the pain is severe enough to disrupt your daily routines and well-being

and reduce swelling. Mix a few heaping tablespoons into the bathwater and soak. More localized soaks are sometimes necessary, especially for the feet. Rest painful feet in a tub of warm water combined with 2 tablespoons Epsom salts. Relax for 15 minutes, pat your tootsies dry, and massage them with your favorite lotion.

FROM THE REFRIGERATOR

DAIRY PRODUCTS. Some medicines used to treat arthritis can lead to a loss of calcium from the bones, resulting in osteoporosis. To counteract this effect (and to keep healthy in general) make sure you get enough calcium in your diet. A cup of low-fat yogurt, for instance, supplies 300 to 400 mg calcium—about one-third of your daily requirement. Calcium-fortified orange juice will also help you meet your daily calcium needs.

FOOD. Decreasing arthritis pain and stiffness may be as easy as eliminating certain foods from your diet. However, the deduction process is a bit difficult, requiring time and observation. There are no set guidelines for this remedy. Rather, it is intuitive. Do you ache more after eating a certain food? Keep a food diary, record what you've eliminated from your diet that week, and rate your discomfort level. There are no guarantees, but you may discover that certain foods contribute to stiffness.

GAMMA LINOLENIC ACID. Recent research suggests that taking high doses of an omega-6 essential fatty acid, known as gamma linolenic acid (GLA), can help reduce joint inflammation. You'll find GLA in some plant seed oils, such as evening primrose and borage, and in black currants. You can also take GLA supplements; 1,800 mg a day is recommended for rheumatoid arthritis. Research also indicates that the benefits of GLA may be enhanced by supplementation with omega-3 fatty acids, which are plentiful in cold-water fish.

FROM THE SINK

HOT AND COLD COMPRESSES. Hot and cold compresses are the simplest remedies for relieving stiff and painful joints. Which to choose depends on what feels good to you… and may depend on the temperature outside. Heat—in the form of a hot, moist towel—combats pain by relaxing muscles and joints and decreasing stiffness. A heating pad or a warm bath or shower will also do the trick. Cold compresses put the chill on joints "hot" from inflammation, which is common with rheumatoid arthritis. Cold helps, too, when you need to pinpoint a specific joint for pain relief. Constructing a cold compress is as easy as running cold water in the sink and soaking a washcloth in it. You can also fill up a plastic bag with crushed ice or use a frozen package of vegetables (peas are perfect). If you use ice, wrap the cold pack in a towel to prevent developing a "freezer burn" on your skin. Apply to sore spots.

FROM THE SUPPLEMENT SHELF

CALCIUM. The Recommended Daily Allowance is 1,000 mg calcium per day for women prior to menopause and 1,200 to 1,500 mg after menopause. Men require 800 mg per day. If you don't get enough calcium in your diet, be sure to supplement to protect your bones.

GLUCOSAMINE. Glucosamine supplements, often found in products that contain a combination of glucosamine and chondroitin, help relieve the pain and may slow the joint degeneration associated with osteoarthritis. The recommended dosage is 500 mg of glucosamine three times a day. It usually takes two to three months of supplementation for maximum benefit.

MORE DO'S AND DON'TS

- Kitchen cures don't only come from the cupboard or refrigerator. Little adjustments in the kitchen itself may make a big difference in protecting arthritic joints from injury or excessive strain.

- Buy kitchen drawer knobs with long, thin handles. These require a looser, less stressful grip.

- More padding means less pain. On tools that require a grip, such as brooms and mops, tape a layer of thin foam rubber around the handles and fasten with tape.

- Use lightweight pots and pans with comfortable handles.

- Utilize a pair of long-handled pinchers (or a gripper) to pick up objects on the floor.

- Transport groceries or heavy items from car to kitchen using a wagon or cart.

- Tie loops made of soft but strong and flame-resistant fabric or rope to the refrigerator and oven doors so you can pull them open without straining.

Bronchitis
CONTROLLING THE COUGH

That nasty cold has been hanging on much longer than it should, and day by day it seems to be getting worse. Your chest hurts, you gurgle when you breathe, and you're coughing so much yellow, green, or grey mucus that your throat is raw. These symptoms are letting you know 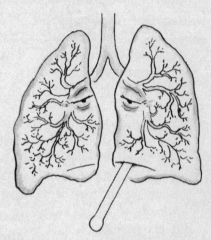 that your cold has probably turned into a respiratory infection called bronchitis, an inflammation of the little branches and tubes of your windpipe that makes them swell. No wonder breathing has become such a chore. Your air passages are too puffy to carry air very easily.

Acute bronchitis can include some or all of these other symptoms, too:

• Wheezing

• Shortness of breath

• Fever or chills

• General aches and pains

• Upper chest pain

WHEN TO CALL THE DOCTOR

- If symptoms last more than three to four days
- If your bronchitis keeps returning
- If the person with bronchitis is an infant or an older adult. Complications in these people can become very serious or even deadly.
- If you have a lot of greenish mucus. You may need antibiotics.
- If you have lung or heart disease, or any other debilitating chronic illness or immune problem
- If you cough up blood. Tiny bright red specks normally come from irritation to the airways, so a few specks of blood can be normal. Coughing up larger amounts or blood that is dried and brownish may require treatment.
- If you have a 102°F temperature for several days

Bronchitis is not contagious since it's a secondary infection that develops when your immune system is weakened by a cold or the flu. Some people are prone to developing it, some are not. Those at the top of the risk list have respiratory problems already, such as asthma, allergies, and emphysema. People who have a weakened immune system also are more prone to bronchitis. But anyone can develop it, and most people do at one time or another.

Ordinarily, bronchitis will go away on its own once the primary infection is cured. But in those few days when you have it, it can sure be miserable. Here are a few kitchen tips that can relieve some of the symptoms.

FROM THE CUPBOARD

ALMONDS. These little cure-all nuts have loads of vitamins and nutrients, and they are known to help everything from mental acuity to sexual vitality. Rich in potassium, calcium, and magnesium, almonds are especially known for their healing powers in respiratory illness. So when you're down with bronchitis, eat them in any form, except candy-coated or chocolate-covered. How about a little almond cream drizzled over your oatmeal? See the Recipe Box, page 35, for this delicious and easy, though caloric, treat. Or sliver some almonds and garnish your veggies. They're good in a citrus fruit salad for a little added crunch or rubbed in a little honey, coated with cinnamon, and roasted in a 325°F oven for 10 to 25 minutes.

COFFEE. The xanthine derivatives in coffee are good bronchodilators. To cut down on mucus problems, add 1 teaspoon apple cider vinegar and 2 drops peppermint oil to a cup of black coffee, either instant or brewed. Drink 1 cup in the morning and evening.

HONEY. To relieve the cough that comes from bronchitis, slice an onion into a bowl, then cover with honey. Allow to stand overnight, then remove the onion. Take 1 teaspoon of the honey four times a day.

SALT. Make a saltwater gargle by mixing 1 teaspoon salt into a glass of warm water. The gargle is soothing, and it can cut down on annoying mucus that's difficult to clear out of the throat. Just be sure not to use more salt, as it can burn your throat, or less salt, as it will be ineffective.

FROM THE REFRIGERATOR

HORSERADISH. The irritating allyl isothiocyanates (mustard derivatives) in horseradish open up the sinuses. Be careful not to use horseradish if you're having stomach problems, though, because it's too potent. Eat it straight, on a salad, or atop meat. Fresh horseradish is the best choice, but commercial products will work, too. Make sure it's straight horseradish, though. Sandwich spreads with horseradish won't work.

LEMONS. These help rid the respiratory system of bacteria and mucus. Make a cup of lemon tea by grating 1 teaspoon lemon rind and adding it to 1 cup boiling water. Steep for five minutes. Or, you can boil a lemon wedge. Strain into a cup and drink. For a sore throat that comes from coughing, add 1 teaspoon lemon juice to 1 cup warm water and gargle. This helps bring up phlegm.

ONIONS. These are expectorants and help the flow of mucus. Use raw, cooked, baked, in soups and stews, as seasoning, or any which way you like them.

FROM THE SINK

WATER. Lots and lots of it. The more you drink, the more your mucus will liquify. This makes it easier to cough out. You can also use water for a steam treatment. Fill the sink with boiling water, bend down to it, cover your head with a towel, and breathe in the steam. Add a few drops of eucalyptus, peppermint, or rosemary oil if you have one of them. These help clear and soothe the respiratory passages.

FROM THE SPICE RACK

ANISEED. Here's a bronchitis cough reliever that's also said to bring on breast milk and relieve heartburn. Boil 1 quart water, then add 7 teaspoons aniseed. Simmer until the water is half gone, strain the seeds, and add 4 teaspoons each of honey and glycerine (glycerine is available at the drugstore). Take 2 teaspoons every few hours.

Bay leaf. Ancient Romans and Greeks loved bay leaves. They believed that this simple herb was the source of happiness, clairvoyance, and artistic inspiration. Whatever the case, it does act as an expectorant and is best taken in tea. To make the tea, tear a leaf (fresh or dried) and steep in 1 cup boiling water. *Warning!* Bay leaf tea should not be used during pregnancy, as it may bring on menstruation. Another bronchitis remedy with bay leaf is to soak some leaves in hot water and apply as a poultice to the chest. Cover with a kitchen towel. As it cools, rewarm.

Ginger. This is a potent expectorant that works well in tea. Steep ½ teaspoon ginger, a pinch of ground cloves, and a pinch of cinnamon in 1 cup boiling water.

Mustard. The warmth of an old-fashioned mustard plaster relieves symptoms of many respiratory ailments, including bronchitis. Take 1 tablespoon dry mustard and mix with 4 tablespoons flour. Stir in enough warm water to make a runny paste. Oil the chest with vegetable short-

Recipe Box

Almond Cream

4 ounces whole almonds
¼ teaspoon pure vanilla extract (increase to ½ if you're using imitation)
honey
cinnamon (optional)

Blanch almonds by covering with ½ cup plus 2 tablespoons water and bringing to a boil. Remove the skins, then puree the almonds in the blender with the water in which they cooked. Add vanilla. Add a pinch of cinnamon (optional). Sweeten to taste with a little honey.

Makes about 1 cup

ening or olive oil, then spread the mustard mix on a piece of cloth—muslin, gauze, a kitchen washcloth—and cover with an identical piece. Apply to the chest. Keep in place until cool, but check every few minutes to make sure it doesn't burn the skin. Remove the plaster if it causes discomfort or burning.

SAVORY. This potent, peppery herb is said to rid the lungs of mucus. Use it as a tea by adding ½ teaspoon savory to 1 cup boiling water. Drink only once a day.

THYME. This herb helps rid the body of mucus, strengthens the lungs to fight off infection, and acts as a shield against bacteria. Use it dried as a seasoning or make a tea by adding ¼ to ½ teaspoon thyme (it's a very strong herb, so you don't need much) to 1 cup boiling water. Steep for 5 minutes and sweeten with honey. If you have thyme oil on hand, dilute it (2 parts olive or corn oil to 1 part thyme oil) and rub on the chest to cure congestion.

FROM THE STOVE

HUMIDITY. You don't need a humidifier to get moisture into your lungs. In fact, because humidifiers can cause as many problems as they cure, this is a better solution: Simmer a pot of water on the stove to send some steam into the atmosphere, which will kill germs and viruses. Or better yet, use a tea kettle: It's designed to shoot out that warm, moist air. Adding a few drops of peppermint or eucalyptus oil can help relieve congestion.

MORE DO'S & DON'TS

• Rest up. Then rest some more. Since bronchitis is usually the second half of a double-illness whammy, your body needs all the rest it can get to build up its strength.

- Don't take a cough suppressant unless your doctor prescribes it. Coughing is your body's way of getting rid of mucus. Mucus buildup can lead to serious respiratory complications such as pneumonia, so when you're congested, that cough is your friend!

- Stay out of harm's way. With bronchitis you're at risk for picking up another infection. Avoid crowds, children with colds, smoky rooms, and contact with anyone who has a cold or flu. Wear gloves or a mask if you have to.

- Wash your hands often: after using a pay phone, handling a contaminated tissue, or shaking hands with someone who may have a cold or a virus.

- Pamper yourself. Go to bed, read a book, listen to music, watch an old movie. Don't be tempted to go about business as usual just because bronchitis isn't usually contagious or serious.

BRONCHITIS-FRIENDLY FOODS

These won't cure, but studies indicate that foods rich in these nutrients may protect against another bout of bronchitis. The more vegetables you eat, the more protection you have.

BETA CAROTENE	VITAMIN E	VITAMIN A	OMEGA-3 FATTY ACIDS
carrots	avocados	mackerel	herring
sweet potatoes	green leafy	canned red	kippers
apricots	veggies	salmon	mackerel
mangoes	whole-grain	anchovies	salmon
green veggies	cereal	whole milk	sardines
		cheese	trout
		egg yolks	fresh tuna
			crab

Burns
PUTTING OUT THE FIRE

The home is one hot place. Just look at all those things heating up in your kitchen: the stove, the oven, the toaster, the microwave, and the waffle iron. Add to that electrical currents and harsh cleaning chemicals and you have plenty of ways to get toasted.

Doctors classify burns by degree. First-degree burns affect the outer layer of skin, called the epidermis. These burns cause pain and redness, but no blistering. Most household burns and sunburns are first degree, and most often they can be treated at home.

Second-degree burns go deeper, involving the epidermis and the dermis, the underlying skin layer. Fluid leaks from damaged blood vessels and causes blistering. These burns are very painful but usually aren't serious unless they are large or become infected. Some second-degree burns can be treated at home; however, if the burn is large or involves the face, hands, feet, or genitals, seek medical attention.

The most serious of all are third-degree burns, which require immediate medical attention. Deep and damaging, this burn involves the outer and inner layers of skin and leaves a path of destruction. Hair, nerves, blood vessels, glands, fat, and even muscle and bone can be damaged. The burn appears white or black and is generally painless since nerves have been destroyed. Third-degree burns often result in death, especially when they cover large areas of the body.

The following remedies only cover minor household burns. Blistering or infected burns, third-degree burns, and chemical or electrical burns require medical attention.

FROM THE CUPBOARD

HONEY. If you're suffering from a burn, the treatment should at least be sweet. Honey has long been a folk remedy to disinfect wounds and heal burns. It forms a protective barrier, kills germs, reduces inflammation, and speeds the growth of healthy tissue. Honey also draws out fluids from the tissues, effectively cleaning the wound. You may apply honey to a gauze bandage, which is less sticky than direct application. On a piece of sterile gauze, place a dollop of honey and apply the bandage directly to the burn, honey-side down. Change the dressing three to four times a day.

OATMEAL. As minor burns heal, they can become itchy. A good way to relieve the itch is by putting this breakfast cereal into the tub. Crumble 1 cup uncooked oatmeal into a bath of lukewarm water as the tub is filling. Soak 15 to 20 minutes, and then air dry so that a thin coating of oatmeal remains on your skin. Use caution getting in and out

WHEN TO CALL THE DOCTOR

- If someone has experienced a third-degree burn
- If the burn is large or involves the face, hands, feet, or genitals
- If the burn blisters severely
- If someone has suffered an electrical or chemical burn
- If the pain and itching get worse after the first 24 hours
- If the victim develops chills or a fever and feels weak

of the tub since the oatmeal makes surfaces slippery.

SALT. Minor mouth burns can be relieved by rinsing with salt water every hour or so. Mix ½ teaspoon salt in 8 ounces warm water.

TEA BAGS. Teatime can be anytime you suffer a minor burn. The tannic acid found in black tea helps draw heat from a burn. Put 2 to 3 tea bags under a spout of cool water and collect the tea in a small bowl. Gently dab the liquid on the burn site.

Another method is to make a concoction using 3 or 4 tea bags, 2 cups fresh mint leaves, and 4 cups boiling water. Strain liquid into a jar and allow to cool. To use, dab the mixture on burned skin with a cotton ball or washcloth.

If you're on the go, you can also make a stay-in-place poultice out of 2 or 3 wet tea bags. Simply place cool wet tea bags directly on the burn and wrap them with a piece of gauze to hold them in place.

VINEGAR. Vinegar works as an astringent and antiseptic on minor burns and helps prevent infection. Dilute the vinegar with equal parts water, and rinse the burned area with the solution.

FROM THE FREEZER

ICE CUBE. A tongue burn is best treated with ice rather than cool water. Often, in great anticipation, children (and adults for that matter) sip their soup or hot chocolate before it cools down and get a tongue burn. Since it's tricky to stick a burned tongue under the faucet, try sucking on an ice cube. First rinse the cube under water so it doesn't stick to the tongue or lips.

FROM THE REFRIGERATOR

MILK. Got milk? Then you've also got a great way to soothe a burn. For a minor burn, soak the burned area in milk for 15 minutes or so. You may also apply a cloth soaked in milk to the area. Repeat every few hours to relieve pain. Be sure to wash out the cloth after use, as it will sour quickly.

PLANTAIN LEAVES. In the folk medicine of the Seneca Indians, as well as the contemporary writing of New Englanders and the Hispanics of the American Southwest, plantain is a popular remedy for treating burns. These green weedy plants *(plantago major)* are native to Europe and Asia but now grow practically anywhere in the world with sufficient water. Just don't confuse this plantain with the bananalike vegetable of the same name.

Plantain leaves are used primarily as medicine. Their major constituents are mucilage, iridoid glycosides (particularly aucubin), and tannins. Together these constituents are thought to give plantain mild anti-inflammatory, antimicrobial, antihemorrhagic, and expectorant actions. To get the full effect of this plant, crush some fresh plantain leaves and rub the juice directly onto the burn.

BUTTER ISN'T BETTER

Many folk remedies have you smearing butter on burns like you would on bread. But butter, or any grease for that matter, should never be applied to burns. First, that butter in the back of your refrigerator isn't sterile. Second, the grease will insulate the burn and hold in the heat. It's best to leave butter for your toast.

FROM THE SINK

COOL WATER. While ice is nice for sore muscles, cool water is the best liquid refreshment for burned skin. Ice can restrict blood flow to the burn site and further damage delicate tissues. Instead, gently run cool water or place cool compresses over the burn site for 10 minutes. Cool water not only feels good but will help stop the burn from spreading.

MORE DO'S AND DON'TS

The kitchen is the number one location for burns, so take the following precautions to prevent an accident:

- Lower the temperature of your hot-water heater to below 120°F. A second-degree burn can happen within seconds in water hotter than 120 degrees.

- Turn pot handles inward on the stove.

- Keep that steaming cup of java out of a child's reach, which means off low-lying furniture.

- Cover all electrical outlets with specially made caps if children are present.

- Never leave a child unattended in the kitchen.

- Put a childproof lock on the oven.

- Keep a fire extinguisher and a box of baking soda (for grease fires) nearby in case of fire.

Colds

SNUFFING OUT THE SNIFFLES

Every year Americans will suffer through more than one billion colds. That's one billion runny noses, coughs, sneezes, aches, and sore throats. Colds make such frequent appearances that the infection has come to be known as the "common cold."

Small children are the most likely to catch a cold: Most kids will have six to ten colds a year. That's because their young immune systems combined with the germy confines of school and day-care situations make them prime targets for the virus. The upside of having so many colds as a child is that you develop immunities to some of the 200 viruses that cause colds. As a result, adults get an average of only two to four colds a year. By the time most people reach age 60, they're down to about one cold per year. Women, especially those between 20 and 30 years old, get more colds than men.

How Do Colds Beat a Path to Your Nose?

Viruses are like a bully that torments kids on the playground. After entering the mucous layer of your nose and

WHEN TO CALL THE DOCTOR

Colds generally have to run their course, typically 2 to 14 days. Rarely, they can lead to a more serious infection. Call your doctor if you have

- High fever
- Severe pain in the chest, ears, head, or stomach
- Enlarged lymph nodes (glands in the neck)
- A fever, sore throat, or severe runny nose that doesn't get any better in a week
- A headache and stiff neck but no other symptoms (could be meningitis)
- A headache and sore throat but no other symptoms (could be strep throat)
- Cold symptoms and pain across your nose and face that sticks around (could be a sinus infection)
- Lessening cold symptoms but then the sudden onset of fever (could be pneumonia)

throat, the cold virus strong-arms your cells until they let the virus take over, forcing the cells to produce thousands of new virus particles.

But the virus is not the reason your throat begins throbbing and your nose starts flowing like Niagara Falls. Your immune system is responsible for that. As the virus begins replicating, the body gets the message that it's time to go into battle. The little soldiers of the body, the white blood cells, run to the body's rescue. One of the weapons the white blood cells use in their virus war are immune system chemicals called kinins. During the battle the kinins tell the body to go into defensive mode. So that runny nose is really your body fighting back against the cursed virus. That should make you feel a little better while you lie on the couch surrounded by tissues.

Because there are so many viruses that cause colds, the

exact virus that you contracted is not easily pinned down. The most likely culprit in most colds is a rhinovirus (rhino is a Greek word meaning "nose"). There are over 110 specific rhinoviruses, and they are behind 30 to 35 percent of colds. The second most common reason for that aching head is a coronavirus. These are especially common in adults, and they cause about 10 to 20 percent of all adult colds. An unknown viral assailant causes 30 to 50 percent of colds.

How Colds Are Spread

The cold virus can take many routes to its ultimate destination—your cells. Most people are contagious a day before and two to four days after their symptoms start. There are typically three ways a cold virus is spread:

- Touching someone who has the virus on them. The virus can live for three hours on skin.

- Touching something that contains the virus. Cold viruses can live three hours on objects.

- Inhaling the virus through airborne transmission. It may sound implausible, but if someone sitting next to you sneezes while you are inhaling, voilà! It's likely you'll get a cold.

One study found that kids tend to get colds from more direct contact while adults tend to get colds from airborne viruses (moms of young children can expect to get colds both ways). Research has also found that emotional stress, allergies that affect the nasal passages or throat, and certain times of the menstrual cycles may make you more susceptible to catching a cold.

Where's the Cold Vaccine?

Good question! One of the main reasons we don't yet have a vaccine for colds is that they're just too hard to pin down. Viruses live inside cells, which means they are protected from most medicines in the bloodstream. So even if you took an antiviral drug, chances are your body wouldn't allow it to penetrate the cells. Another reason viruses are so difficult to kill is that they don't grow well in a laboratory setting. Their ultimate playground is a warm, dry place, just like the inside of your nose.

Don't give up hope, though. Researchers are still on the job. They have discovered the receptor sites that the rhinovirus attaches to when it invades a cell. They tested an antibody that blocked these receptor sites and helped slow down the time the virus actually took to develop into a cold. It also reduced the severity of its symptoms.

While colds are here to stay for now, you don't have to be totally at their mercy. Thankfully, there are some things you can do to fend off the germs that cause colds, as well as techniques to ease your symptoms once you're sick.

FROM THE CUPBOARD

CHICKEN SOUP. Science actually backs up what your mom knew all along—chicken soup does help a cold. Scientists believe it's the fumes in the soup that release the mucus in your nose and help your body better fight against its viral invaders. Chicken soup also contains cysteines, which are good at thinning mucus. And the soup provides easily absorbed nutrients.

CORN SYRUP. You can make a sugar-water gargle to ease your throat. Use 1 tablespoon syrup per 8 ounces warm water, mix together, then gargle.

HONEY. Make your own cough syrup by mixing together ¼ cup honey and ¼ cup apple cider vinegar. Pour the mixture into a jar or bottle and seal tightly. Shake well before using. Take 1 tablespoon every four hours.

SALT. Make your own saline nose drops by adding ¼ teaspoon salt to 8 ounces water. You can also make a saltwater gargle for your sore throat with the same ratio of salt to water. Salt is an astringent and helps relieve a painful throat.

SESAME OIL. Dry nasal passages are prime breeding grounds for the cold virus. Although doctors typically recommend saline nose drops during the winter to keep nasal passages moist, a recent study compared saline drops to sesame oil. The people who used sesame oil had an 80 percent improvement in their nasal dryness while the people who used traditional saline drops had a 30 percent

YOU CAN'T CATCH A COLD FROM THE COLD

Cold weather may make you uncomfortable, but it doesn't make you more susceptible to getting a cold. There are two reasons colds tend to make more of an impact in cold weather. Number one, most people are indoors a lot more in the winter, so you've got a lot more opportunities to share the wealth of cold viruses. And number two, the heat in your house dries out the air, and cold viruses like it warm and dry. So if you throw a little wintertime soiree in your well-heated home, you've got the ideal climate for a cold virus. Scientists have done numerous tests in which they've exposed people to the cold virus in 86°F and 40°F temperatures, and much to the participants' chagrin, both groups ended up with a cold.

improvement. While it may not be a good idea to shoot sesame oil up your nose (it could get into the lungs), try rubbing a drop around the inside of your nostrils.

TEA. A cup of hot tea with honey does the same trick as chicken soup; it loosens up your nasal passages and makes that stuffy nose feel better. Folk healers have known this secret for centuries. They often suggest drinking tea with spices and herbs that contain aromatic oils with antiviral properties. Try tea with elder, ginger, yarrow, mint, thyme, horsemint, bee balm, lemon balm, catnip, garlic, onions, or mustard.

FROM THE REFRIGERATOR

PEPPERS. Hot and spicy foods are notorious for making your nose run and your eyes water. The hot stuff in peppers is called capsaicin and is pharmacologically similar to guaifenesin, an expectorant found in some over-the-counter cough syrups. This similarity leads some experts to believe that eating hot foods can clear up mucus and ease that stuffy nose.

YOGURT. One study found that participants who ate ¾ cup yogurt a day before and during cold season had 25 percent fewer colds. But you've got to start early and maintain your yogurt eating throughout the peak cold season.

FROM THE SUPPLEMENT SHELF

VITAMIN C. Vitamin C won't prevent a cold, but research shows that it can help reduce the length and severity of symptoms. But to reap the benefits, you've got to take a lot of "C." The RDA for men and women 15 and older is 60 mg, but studies show that you'd need to take upward of 1,000 mg to 3,000 mg to get the cold-symptom-sparing rewards of vitamin C. For the short term, experts believe that wouldn't be harmful, but taking too much vitamin C for too long can cause severe diarrhea. Before loading up on vitamin C, check with your doctor.

ZINC. Studies have found that zinc may help immune cells fight a cold and may ease cold symptoms. The most effective zinc lozenges are those that contain 15 to 25 mg of zinc gluconate or zinc gluconate-glycine per lozenge. You can get the most out of your zinc lozenges if you start using them at the first sign of a cold and continue taking them for several days.

MORE DO'S AND DON'TS

- Don't fix yourself a hot toddy; they don't work. Alcohol can make you more stuffy. Best to avoid it while you've got a cold.

- Don't smoke. Smokers tend to have longer colds, and they're more likely to end up with complications, such as bronchitis.

- Don't take antibiotics. Antibiotics don't fight viral infections, so they aren't effective against colds. And taking too many antibiotics can help foster the growth and spread of antiobiotic-resistant germs that can cause much more serious infections.

- Keep your chin up. Just as emotional stress can wear your immune system down, having a positive attitude can help you win the war against your cold.

Cold Sores
MINIMIZING THE MISERY

You know it's coming when you feel that notorious tingling on your lip and the accompanying itching and burning. You can't help stressing out about it; all you can think about is the pain and embarrassment those ugly cold sores cause. But there's not a darned thing you can do to stop a cold sore, also known as a fever blister, from erupting.

Many people get confused about whether they have a cold sore or a canker sore. But that confusion is easily cleared up. If the sore is on your external lip or near your mouth or nose and looks like a fluid-filled blister, chances are it's a cold sore. Caused by a virus called herpes simplex Type 1, herpes blisters are very contagious. They also love company, so where there's one there are usually many. Within a few days to a week, the blisters break, ooze, and form an ugly yellow crust that can stay around for weeks. When the scab finally sloughs off, though, there's nice, healthy pink skin underneath. Best of all, cold sores leave no scars.

You can't cure cold sores, and they like to keep coming back, usually to the scene of a previous visit. When a cold sore's not making itself a huge lip ache, it's snoozing in the nerves below your skin, just waiting to be awakened. What sets off its alarm clock?

- Fever
- Infection, colds, flu
- Ultraviolet radiation, such as a sunburn
- Stress
- Fatigue
- Changes in the immune system
- Trauma or irritation
- Food allergies
- Menstruation
- Dental work

WHEN TO CALL THE DOCTOR

- If your eyes hurt or you have vision problems while you have the cold sore
- If you have a fever of 100°F or more
- If you develop chills
- If the sores don't heal on their own within 7 to 10 days
- If sores come back frequently
- If you suspect you may have infected your genitals

Who's Prone?

Anyone who comes in contact with the herpes simplex virus can catch it. It is spread in air droplets and by direct contact with fluid from the blister. Those at highest risk have a weakened immune system and a family history of cold sores.

Conventional medicine does have a few tricks in its little black bag, including antiviral lotions and creams. But they don't cure, just treat. So take a look in your kitchen. You might just find some useful treatments there, too.

FROM THE CANDY JAR

LICORICE. Studies show that glycyrrhizic acid, an ingredient in licorice, stops the cold sore virus cells dead in their tracks. So try chewing a licorice whip. Just be sure it's made from real licorice, as most candy in the United States today is flavored with anise. If the ingredient list says "licorice mass," the product contains real licorice. You could also try buying some licorice powder and sprinkling it on the sore. Or mix up a cream with a pinch of licorice power and a smidgen of pure vegetable shortening, then apply to the sore.

FROM THE FREEZER

ICE PACKS. If you ice a cold sore when it first arrives, you may cut down on the amount of time it hangs around. Ice packs and cold compresses will provide some temporary relief. A tasty popsicle will feel good, too, but skip the juice bars. Their acid content may irritate that major irritation even more. Super-cold drinks such as slushes or smoothies are another tasty way to provide comfort.

FROM THE REFRIGERATOR

MILK. This remedy doesn't involve drinking. Soak a cotton ball in milk and apply it to the sore to relieve pain. Better yet, if you feel the tell-tale tingling before the cold sore surfaces, go straight to the cold milk. It can help speed the healing right from the beginning.

MORE DO'S AND DON'TS

- Change toothbrushes: once when the blister has formed and once when the attack has cleared up. Toothbrushes can harbor the virus.

- Don't kiss. Whether it's you or your partner with the cold sore, don't give any smooches. In fact, don't even make skin contact when blisters are present.

- Reduce your stress. Exercise, meditate, try yoga, read a good book.

- Don't share drinks, foods, utensils, towels, or anything that may have come in contact with a moist secretion from the blister.

- Don't touch other parts of your body (or anybody else's

FOODS THAT FIGHT COLD SORES

There's a good amino acid, lysine, that helps block the herpes virus. So try some foods high in this cold sore warrior, such as:

- Meats
- Milk
- Fish
- Chicken
- Eggs
- Beans & bean sprouts
- Cheese

Foods rich in bioflavonoids can help prevent or speed up the course of the blisters that flare up, too. These include

- Onions
- Apples
- Grapes
- Tea

Foods packed with vitamin C are also valiant in their quest to rid you of your herpes foe. Eat a lot of these vitamin C-rich foods:

- Oranges, grapefruits, seedless berries
- Peppers
- Green leafy vegetables

- Sweet potatoes, potatoes

body) without first washing your hands. Cold sores can spread to your eyes and your genitals, so wash your hands frequently or that little lip sore could turn into something much worse.

- Use a strong sunblocking lip protectant whenever you go outside during the day.

- Don't hide your boo-boo with makeup. The chemicals can make the sore worse. And don't share your lipstick or other makeup either.

- Don't squeeze, pinch, or pick a blister. These actions can cause a bacterial infection.

- Suck on zinc lozenges. During stressful times they can boost the immune system.

- Carry hand sanitizer in case you accidentally scratch and there's no sink handy.

Constipation
Getting a Move On

Nothing's moving, but you know you have to "go." Everything in your body is sending you that signal. You feel bloated and have uncomfortable pressure, but when you try to move your bowels, nothing happens. Or, if you do finally go, it hurts.

Constipation occurs for many different reasons. Stress, lack of exercise, certain medications, artificial sweeteners, and a diet that's lacking fiber or fluids—any of these can be the culprit. Certain medical conditions such as an underactive thyroid, irritable bowel syndrome, diabetes, and cancer can also cause constipation. Even age is a factor. The older we get, the more prone we are to this annoying problem.

And constipation is a problem, although it's not an illness. It's simply what happens when bowel movements are delayed, compacted, and difficult to pass.

What's Normal?

Some people mistakenly believe they must have a certain number of bowel movements a day or a week or

WHEN TO CALL THE DOCTOR

- If you have fever or lower abdominal pain with constipation
- If you have blood in your stools
- If constipation develops after you start taking a new medication. This includes vitamins and minerals.
- If you're elderly or disabled and you've been constipated for more than a week
- If you experience sudden weight loss with constipation
- If the problem persists, off and on, for more than two weeks
- If you're experiencing extreme pain and discomfort
- If constipation is causing a problem with normal daily activities
- If you experience a marked change in your normal bowel habits

else they are constipated. That couldn't be further from the truth, although it's a common misconception. What constitutes "normal" is individual and can vary from three bowel movements a day to three a week. You'll know if you're constipated because you'll be straining a lot in the bathroom, you'll produce unusually hard stools, and you'll feel gassy and bloated.

Don't Reach for Laxatives Right Away

It's not a good idea to use laxatives as the first line of attack when you're constipated. They can become habit-forming to the point that they damage your colon. Some laxatives inhibit the effectiveness of medications you're already taking, and there are laxatives that cause inflammation to the lining of the intestine.

Conventional thinking on laxatives is that if you must take one, find one that's psyllium- or fiber-based. Psyllium is a natural fiber that's much more gentle on the system than ingredients in many of the other products available today. Or, simply look in the kitchen for relief. It's there.

FROM THE CUPBOARD

BARLEY. It can relieve constipation as well as keep you regular, and it has cholesterol-lowering properties, too. What more could you ask of a simple grain? Buy some barley flour, flakes, and grits. Add some barley grain to vegetable soup or stew.

BLACKSTRAP MOLASSES. Take 2 tablespoons before going to bed. It has a pretty strong taste, so you may want to add it to milk, fruit juice, or for an extra-powerful laxative punch, prune juice.

GARLIC. In the raw, it has a laxative effect for many. Eat it mixed with onion, raw or cooked, and with milk or yogurt for best results.

HONEY. This is a very mild laxative. Try taking 1 table-spoon three times a day, either by itself or mixed into warm water. If it doesn't work on its own, you can pep it up by mixing it half and half with blackstrap molasses.

OIL. Safflower, soybean, or other vegetable oil can be just the cure you need, as each has a lubricating action in the intestines. Take 2 to 3 tablespoons a day until the problem is gone. If you don't like taking it straight, mix the oil with herbs and lemon juice or vinegar to use as salad dressing. The combination of the oil and the fiber from the salad ought to fix you right up.

VINEGAR. Mix 1 teaspoon apple cider vinegar and 1 tea-spoon honey in a glass of water and drink.

WALNUTS. Fresh from the shell, they may be just the laxative you need.

FROM THE REFRIGERATOR

APPLE JUICE, APPLE CIDER. These are natural laxatives for many people. Drink up and enjoy!

APPLES. Eat an hour after a meal to prevent constipation.

BANANAS. These may relieve constipation. Try eating two ripe bananas between meals. Avoid green bananas because they're constipating.

PRUNES. Yep, they work! And here's a great-tasting way to cure constipation. Cover several prunes with boiling water. If you wish to sweeten the prunes, stir 1 or 2 teaspoons honey into the boiling water before you pour it over the fruit. Let the prunes stand in the water overnight, and eat them the next day. Drink the prune juice, too. This works with figs, as well.

RAISINS. Eat a handful daily, an hour after a meal.

RHUBARB. This is a natural laxative. Cook it and eat it sweetened with honey or bake it in a pie. Or, create a drink with cooked, pureed rhubarb, apple juice, and honey.

FROM THE SPICE RACK

SESAME SEED. These provide roughage and bulk, and they soften the contents of the intestines, which makes elimination easier. Eat no more than ½ ounce daily, and drink lots of water as you take the seeds. You may also sprinkle them on salads and other foods, but again, no more than ½ ounce. Sesame is also available in a butter or paste and in Middle Eastern dips, such as tahini.

MORE DO'S AND DON'TS

- Exercise. A nice, brisk 30-minute walk can lead to regularity.

- Drink at least 8 glasses of water a day.

- Don't rush things. It takes time for your bowels to move, so allow sufficient time.

- Don't take mineral oil unless prescribed by your physician.

- If you suffer frequent bouts of constipation, keep a food diary and see which foods are clogging you up or if fibrous foods are missing.

- Cut back on refined foods, such as processed cereals, white flour, and sugar.

- A movement delayed can result in constipation. In other words, go when nature calls.

HERBAL REMEDIES

You won't necessarily find these in the kitchen cupboard, but if you do, they can help cure that constipation.

Flaxseeds. These provide natural bulk and will relieve constipation. Wash 2 teaspoons seeds in cold water. Add to 1 cup boiling water. Let steep for ten minutes, then drink. Do not strain out the seeds.

Senna. This will work, but children under 12 and women who are pregnant should not use it. Here's the recipe: Place ¼ to ½ teaspoon crushed senna leaves or powder in 1 cup boiling water. Let it steep for ten minutes. Use once a day for no more than ten days.

Warning! Use only a small amount of senna. It's very strong, and one full teaspoonful can cause abdominal cramping.

- A daily routine is best. Train yourself. Pick a time, possibly after a meal, and retire to the bathroom. Follow that routine every day, whether you have to go or not, and soon it may very well become your time.

Cough
HAMPERING THE HACK

Annoying, loud, and disruptive, a persistent cough can put a damper on your daily routine. Coughs can be defined by how long they last. A brief cough is caused by such factors as cold air, irritating fumes, breathing dust, or drawing food into the airways. A persistent cough, however, typically results from mucus and other secretions brought on by respiratory disorders such as the cold, the flu, pneumonia, or tuberculosis.

Moisture content also differentiates coughs. Some are dry, accompanied by a ticklish or sore throat. Others are accompanied by a thick phlegm and are called wet coughs.

A Beneficial Reflex

Regardless of time and moisture content, a cough is produced when viruses, bacteria, dust, pollen, or other foreign substances irritate respiratory passages in the throat and lungs. The cough reflex is the body's effort to rid the passageways of such intruders, and it spares no power in the expulsion. A cough reflex can expel a foreign substance at velocities as high as 100 miles per hour.

Determine what kind of cough you have and search out cures specific to that type. Some remedies aim to moisten dry throats, while others are expectorants, helping you cough up and get rid of mucus and irritants. Most of these kitchen cures aim to battle both coughs unless otherwise noted.

FROM THE CANDY JAR

LICORICE. If you love licorice, you're in for a treat with this remedy. Many folk remedies use licorice root to treat coughs and bronchial problems. It serves not only as a flavoring agent but also as a demulcent (a substance that soothes inflamed or irritated throats) and an expectorant. Real licorice or candy that's actually made with real licorice (look for "licorice mass" on the label) works best. Reach into your candy jar and slice up 1 ounce licorice sticks. Add 1 quart boiling water and steep for 24 hours. Drink throughout the day, adding a teaspoon of honey for sweetness.

WHEN TO CALL THE DOCTOR

- If you have a persistent cough that doesn't improve after ten days of treatment, especially an unexplained cough or one that's dry and hacking
- If you have a cough that produces thick, foul-smelling rusty or greenish phlegm
- If you experience chest pain when you breathe
- If you cough up blood

FROM THE CUPBOARD

GARLIC. Eating garlic won't have you winning any kissing contests, but who wants to kiss you when you sound like a seal? Since kissing isn't on your agenda, you can indulge in one of nature's best cures for coughs: garlic. It's full of antibiotic and antiviral properties, plus garlic is an expectorant, so it helps you cough up stubborn bacteria and/or mucus that are languishing in your lungs.

Some experts advise that to reap garlic's full cold- and flu-fighting benefits, you have to eat it raw. Yet swallowing 4 to 8 raw garlic cloves a day (the recommended amount) is hard for most people to stomach. Cheat a little by mixing the cloves into plain yogurt and putting a dollop on your soup. If you make a pasta sauce, put the garlic in at the last moment, or toss garlic slices into your salad.

A cup of garlic broth may do the trick for your cough, too, and it is easy to prepare. Smash 1 to 3 cloves garlic (depending on how strong you like your garlic), add 2 quarts water, and boil on low heat for one hour. Strain and sip slowly.

You can also chop up some garlic cloves and toss them into that pot of chicken soup (see "From the Stove," page 64) simmering on the stove.

HONEY. Honey has long been used in traditional Chinese medicine for coughs because it's a natural expectorant, promoting the flow of mucus. This is the simple recipe: Mix 1 tablespoon honey into 1 cup hot water and enjoy. Now how sweet is that? Squeeze some lemon juice in if you want a little tartness. Before bedtime, adults may add 1 tablespoon brandy or whiskey to aid in sleep.

FROM THE REFRIGERATOR

GINGER. Ginger, which has antiviral properties, shares the limelight with licorice in this cough remedy. To make ginger-licorice (anise) tea, combine 2 teaspoons freshly chopped gingerroot, 2 teaspoons aniseed, and if available, 1 teaspoon dried licorice root in 2 cups boiling water. Cover and steep for ten minutes. Strain and sweeten with 1 or 2 teaspoons honey. Drink ½ cup every one to two hours, but no more than 3 cups a day.

FROM THE SPICE RACK

MUSTARD SEED. An irritating but useful spice for wet coughs, mustard seed has sulfur-containing compounds that stimulate the flow of mucus. To get the full effect of the expectorant compounds, the mustard seeds must be broken and allowed to sit in water for 15 minutes. Crush 1 teaspoon mustard seeds or grind them in a coffee grinder. Place the seeds in a cup of warm water. Steep for 15 minutes. This concoction might be a little hard to swallow, so take it in ¼-cup doses throughout the day.

PEPPER. Pepper is a bit of an irritant (try sniffing some), but this characteristic is a plus for those suffering from coughs accompanied by thick mucus. The irritating property of pepper stimulates circulation and the flow of mucus in the airways and sinuses. Place 1 teaspoon black pepper into a cup and sweeten things up with the addition of 1 tablespoon honey. Fill with boiling water, steep for 10 to 15 minutes, stir, and sip.

SALT. A saltwater gargle is a simple solution to a cough, although you have to remain devoted to gargling to get results. Mix ¼ teaspoon salt into 4 ounces warm water.

Mix and gargle. Repeat this every one to two hours each day for best results. The salt, combined with soothing warm water, acts as an astringent to help ease irritated and inflamed throat tissues and loosen mucus.

THYME. Store-bought cough syrups are often so medicinal tasting that it's hard to get them down without gagging. Here's a sweet, herbal version, made of thyme, peppermint, mullein, licorice, and honey, that's guaranteed to go down the hatch easily. Thyme and peppermint help clear congested air passages and have antimicrobial and antispasmodic properties to relieve the hacking. Mullein and licorice soothe irritated membranes and help reduce inflammation.

To make the syrup, combine 2 teaspoons each dried thyme, peppermint, mullein, and licorice root into 1 cup boiling water. Cover and steep for half an hour. Strain and add ½ cup honey. If the honey doesn't dissolve, heat the tea gently and stir. Store in the refrigerator in a covered container for up to three months. Take 1 teaspoon as needed.

FROM THE STOVE

CHICKEN SOUP. Take some advice from your grandma: Sip a bowl of chicken soup. It doesn't matter if it's homemade or canned. Chicken soup is calming for coughs associated with colds. While scientists can't put a finger on why this comfort food benefits the cold sufferer, they do believe chicken soup contains anti-inflammatory properties that help prevent a cold's miserable side effects, one being the cough. Plus, chicken soup contains cysteine, which thins phlegm. The broth, chock-full of electrolytes, keeps you hydrated, and the steam helps soothe irritated mucous membranes and air passageways. Last, but not least, it tastes yummy.

STEAM. One of the kitchen's best remedies for a cough is also one of the easiest. Inhaling steam helps flush out mucus, and it moisturizes dry, irritated air passageways. Fill a cooking pot one-quarter full with water. Boil, turn off the heat, and if available, add a couple drops essential oil of eucalyptus or a scoop of Mentholatum or Vicks VapoRub. (These work as decongestants and expectorants.) Carefully remove the pot from the stove, and place it on a protected counter or table. Drape a towel over your head, lean over the pot, and breathe gently for 10 to 15 minutes. Don't stick your face too far into the pot or you'll get a poached nose.

A SOOTHING CHEST RUB

When the chest hurts from coughing fits and breathing is congested, a soothing remedy to loosen and lighten things up is a homemade eucalyptus-lavender chest rub. Eucalyptus, a common ingredient in store-bought vapor balms, opens congested airways and acts as an antimicrobial. Lavender, long regarded as a soothing herb that eases anxiety, also aids slightly in the battle against bad germs and microorganisms. To make a chest rub, combine 10 drops lavender essential oil, 15 drops eucalyptus essential oil, and ¼ cup olive oil or vegetable oil. Mix and massage on your upper chest before getting into bed.

If you'd rather not have an oily chest but want the same benefits, try taking a bath instead. Add 3 drops eucalyptus oil and 3 drops lavender oil to a full warm bath. Soak for ten minutes.

Denture Discomfort
MAKING THE ADJUSTMENT

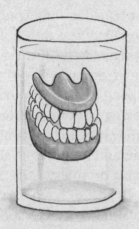

Anyone who has donned a set of dentures knows discomfort is part of the process. There are two periods when discomfort is at its peak: the initial days of wearing the new device and several years later when the dentures may not fit properly.

The cause of the discomfort isn't a mystery. After the teeth are extracted, the dentures sit on the bony ridge that's left over. Without the stability of permanent teeth, this bony ridge changes and shrinks over the years while the dentures remain fixed. Slipping and sliding dentures cause sore spots, which is the reason for much of denture discomfort.

Dentures may not fit like a glove, but you shouldn't suffer. There are a variety of ways to prevent and resolve denture discomfort.

FROM THE REFRIGERATOR

FIGS. Mexicans, Hispanics from the American Southwest, and Arabs think figs are fabulous for fighting mouth sores. The fig remedy, however, requires some time, coordination, and of course, a fresh fig. Once you locate the prized fruit, cut it in half and set one half between your cheek and the sore spot on your gum. The open side of the fig should touch the gum. This is a bit tricky to keep in place, so plan on watching TV or keeping still while you fig out.

SOFT FOODS. Eat like a baby during the adjustment period. You don't have to blend everything, just stick to soft, easy-to-chew foods such as soups, stews, and pastas (such as macaroni and cheese). If you chew on hard foods, such as carrots and pretzels, you'll risk damaging tender gum tissues that are still in shock from losing their natural teeth. For dessert, enjoy puddings, gelatin, and applesauce.

> ## WHEN TO CALL A DENTIST
> - If you develop soreness that doesn't improve within a week
> - If an area on your gum bleeds spontaneously or is filled with pus
> - If you notice extra tissue growing, particularly between the upper lip and the gum
> - If a white sore persists for more than a week
> - If you have a mouth sore that doesn't heal completely in 10 to 14 days

FROM THE SINK

SOAP. After teeth are extracted and new dentures fit, it's of prime importance to keep your new choppers sparkling clean. Excess bacteria buildup on dentures can retard the gum's healing process. Plain old soap, warm water, and a hand brush do a grand job at cleaning. Scrub at least twice a day and rinse well.

FROM THE SPICE RACK

ANISEED. This gentle herbal mouth rinse is perfect for sensitive mouths. Combine 2 teaspoons crushed aniseed, 1

BY GEORGE! I THINK HE'S GOT DENTURES!

The world's most famous denture wearer was the first president of the United States, George Washington. After having all his permanents removed, he was given a pair of hand-carved dentures crafted from hippopotamus and cow teeth. The contraption was held in his mouth by two springs on each side.

Washington suffered, as his false teeth were one size too big, and he eased the pain with hemp extract. His denture-wearing days were also a source of embarrassment. The ill-fitting teeth caused a speech impediment and forced Washington to restrict his diet to babylike foods.

tablespoon peppermint leaves, and 2 cups boiling water. Cover and steep for eight hours. Strain and add 1 teaspoon myrrh tincture, which acts as an antiseptic and preservative. Use 2 tablespoons twice a day for rinsing. The remainder of the rinse can be stored in a glass bottle. Shake before using.

CLOVE. The clove has been used as a remedy for aching mouths since antiquity. The clove remedy started in Asian folk medicine, and the concept traveled along trade routes to Europe and the Mediterranean along with the spice itself. By the third century B.C. the clove was the universal folk remedy for mouth and dental pain in the Mediterranean. Clove's medicinal use continued into the nineteenth century, when dentists used clove oil to relieve dental pain. Even today dentists use eugenol, a major ingredient in clove oil, as a pain reliever and to disinfect dental abscesses. Cloves not only eliminate pain but also smell terrific. To tap into these healing properties, blend 1 teaspoon cloves into a powder using a coffee grinder or use ½ teaspoon prepackaged ground cloves. Moisten with olive oil and dab around a mouth or gum sore.

SALT. Gargling with warm salt water may help denture wearers breeze through the adjustment phase sans mouth sores. Prevent sore spots from becoming infected or inflamed by rinsing every three to four hours. The salt water cleans out bacteria, shrinks swollen tissue, and helps toughen the tender tissue. Make a saltwater rinse by adding ½ teaspoon salt to 4 ounces warm water. Gargle and spit.

MORE DO'S AND DON'TS

- Give your mouth a rest. Always remove your false teeth at night. You may also want to remove dentures for 24 hours should you develop a red spot on the gums.

- Have your dentures checked yearly.

- Have your dentures relined every two to three years.

- Replace dentures every five to six years, depending on the amount of wear and tear and the shrinkage of the gums.

A HEALTHY RINSE

Use a 3-percent solution of hydrogen peroxide as a mouth rinse to keep gums and mouth healthy. Anything stronger than 3 percent is dangerous. Hydrogen peroxide rids the mouth of food particles, and the oxygenating agent helps boost the fighting properties of good bacteria. The rinse also helps act against bad bacteria, although on a more limited basis.

For gargling, dilute hydrogen peroxide with an equal amount of water and swish around your mouth for 30 seconds. Don't swallow the rinse; however, if a drop or two sneaks down your throat, body heat and stomach acid should dissipate it.

Diabetes
CONTROLLING BLOOD SUGAR

Diabetes is a disease that
reduces, or stops, the body's
ability to produce or respond
to insulin, a hormone produced in the pancreas.
Insulin's role is to open
the door for glucose, a
form of sugar, to enter
the body's cells so that
it can be used for energy. When the
body has a problem metabolizing glucose, it builds up in
the blood, and the body's cells starve.

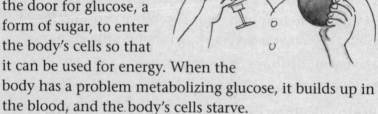

There are two major types of diabetes:

Type 1. The body produces no insulin at all, and daily
insulin shots are required. This disease used to be called
juvenile diabetes because there is a higher rate of diagnosis
among children ages 10 to 14. It is also referred to as
insulin-dependent diabetes because injections of insulin
are required to control blood glucose. The cause isn't
known, but Type 1 tends to run in families. A much
smaller number of people with diabetes have Type 1—
only five percent.

Type 2. This is the most common form of diabetes, and
it occurs when the body is insulin resistant. That could be

either because the body fails to make enough insulin or because it doesn't properly use the insulin it does produce. The cause is often poor dietary habits, sedentary lifestyle, and obesity. Those with Type 2 may or may not need oral medication or insulin, depending on how their body responds to changes in diet and exercise.

Here's the risk list for diabetes. Do any of these describe you?

- Over age 45
- Family history of diabetes
- Overweight
- Don't exercise regularly
- Low HDL cholesterol (see High Cholesterol, page 136) or high triglycerides

WHEN TO CALL THE DOCTOR

If you have not been diagnosed with diabetes, call if one or more of the symptoms in this profile are present. If you have diabetes, call if:

- You vomit or have diarrhea for more than 24 hours
- You can't eat or drink
- Your blood sugar is more than 240 or less than 80 for more than 48 hours
- You run a fever of 101°F or more for two days
- Your vision goes blurry
- You experience other unusual physical symptoms such as weakness or difficulty when speaking
- You have an open sore on your legs or feet

Symptoms

In children, the symptoms of the onset of Type 1 diabetes may be similar to flu symptoms. They also may include these:

- Frequent urination
- Unusual thirst
- Extreme hunger

- Unexplained weight loss
- Extreme fatigue
- Irritability

Symptoms of Type 2 diabetes include:

- Any of the Type 1 symptoms
- Frequent infections, including those of the skin, gums, and bladder
- Blurred vision
- Sores that are slow to heal
- Tingling or numbness in hands or feet
- In women, recurring vaginitis

Treatment

There is no cure for diabetes, but it can be controlled. And control is essential because diabetes can lead to heart disease, stroke, kidney disease and failure, blindness, and amputation if not treated. This profile will not address diabetic medical treatment, including prescribed diabetic diets. Those specifics must be left up to your physician and dietitian. But this profile will cover the go-alongs: things from your kitchen that can make the diabetic experience easier, as well as alternative practices that might help. Before you try any alternative practice, consult your physician. Nothing contained in this profile is intended to stop or replace your prescribed diabetic care!

Diabetes is a complex disease, affecting many parts of the body. Some of the problems of the disease can be relieved with simple things right from the kitchen, though. And for a person with diabetes, a little relief never hurts.

FROM THE CUPBOARD

GARLIC. Eating a combination of garlic, parsley, and watercress may shave a few points off the blood sugar. Try combining these herbs in a vegetable stir-fry or salad.

OLIVE OIL. Studies indicate olive oil may reduce blood sugar levels. Use it in salad dressing or wherever cooking oils are indicated. For an easy no-stick olive oil spray-on coating, buy an oil mister in any department store kitchen supply area and use it to spray your pans before cooking.

PEANUT BUTTER. After you've experienced an episode of low blood sugar and corrected it, follow up with a protein and carbohydrate snack. Peanut butter on a couple of crackers supplies both, and it's easy to fix when you may still feel a little jittery. Just avoid brands that contain added sugar, glucose, or jelly.

PLASTIC CONTAINER. If you're on insulin, keep your extra vials in the refrigerator. Designate a spot where your insulin bottle won't freeze yet is away from the food. Then keep the vial in a plastic container, preferably one that shields it from light, in that spot to keep it from rolling

AN INFORMATIVE TEST

A simple blood test called hemoglobin A1C (also called HbA1C) can measure your cumulative average blood sugar levels for the past three months. It's the best test to find out whether your blood sugar is under control. People with diabetes should have a hemoglobin A1C test at least every six months. The goal is a finding of 7 percent or less. That's because a major diabetes study shows that those whose results were 7 percent or lower had a much better chance of delaying or preventing diabetes complications related to the eyes, kidneys, and nerves than those whose levels were 8 percent or higher.

around or getting knocked aside or misplaced. If the insulin bottle is frosted or the insulin clumps, do not use it. Consult your pharmacist and the package insert for information about proper storage.

SALT. Dry, itchy skin is a side effect of diabetes, and soaking in a tub of salt water can be a great itchy skin reliever. Just add 1 cup table salt or sea salt to your bathwater. This solution will also soften skin and relax you. To exfoliate, after you take a shower or bath and while your skin is still wet, sprinkle salt onto your hands and rub it all over your skin. This salt massage will remove dry skin and make your skin smoother to the touch. It will also invigorate your skin and get your circulation moving. Try it first thing in the morning to help wake up or after a period of physical exertion.

SALTSHAKER. Set it aside, put it back in the cupboard, hide it. High blood pressure is a side effect of diabetes, and salt's a no-no. So don't cook with it, and don't make it handy to grab when you eat a meal or snack. If it's out of sight or inconvenient to get, you might just skip it. Instead, reach for a nice herb or spice blend that's sodium free. Make one yourself with your favorite spices or buy one at the store.

SUGAR. Yes, even people with diabetes need it occasionally, when their blood sugar goes too low. A spoonful of straight sugar will work, as will a piece of hard candy. Just be sure it's not sugarless.

VINEGAR. Muscle cramps, especially in the legs, can affect people with diabetes. To get relief from the ache, add 8 ounces apple cider vinegar to a bathtub of warm water. Soak for at least 15 minutes.

FROM THE DRAWER

FORK. This is how you should apply salad dressing and sauces to limit your intake of sugar, as well as fat and cholesterol. Instead of dumping the dressing or sauce all over your food, have it served "on the side" and dip your fork into it, then pick up your food. You'll get the flavor without all the extra goop.

NOTEBOOK. Use this to keep track of glucose readings, medication schedules, and symptoms.

FASCINATING FACT

According to a Dutch study, fish eaters are half as likely to get Type 2 diabetes as people who don't eat fish. The amount consumed was small—1 ounce a day. Most likely the omega-3 oil found in fish helps the pancreas handle glucose.

FROM THE REFRIGERATOR

ASPARAGUS. This vegetable is a mild diuretic that's said to be beneficial in the control of diabetes. Eat it steamed and drizzled with olive oil and lemon juice.

BEANS. They've been known to reduce blood sugar in some people. Kidney beans are the best, fresh in the pod. Boil 2 ounces of sliced pods in 4 quarts of water. Simmer four hours. Strain and cool the liquid for eight hours. Strain again. Drink 1 glassful every two hours. In the absence of kidney bean pods, fresh green beans will work, too. Beans eaten with a meal, just as they are, have been known to lessen the rise in blood sugar that comes after the meal.

LEMON. A squirt of lemon provides a tasty substitute for salt. And squeezed into a diet cola, it cuts the aftertaste.

PARSLEY. Steep into a tea and drink. This may act as a diuretic to control blood pressure and lower blood sugar.

WATERCRESS. This is said to strengthen the natural defense systems of people who have diabetes. It's also a mild diuretic. Wash the leaves thoroughly and add them to a salad. Or smear a little cream cheese on a slice of bread, then top with watercress for a tasty open-faced sandwich.

MORE DO'S AND DON'TS

- Monitor your glucose levels regularly via finger sticks. That's the only way you can accurately gauge how you're doing. Record the results for your doctor and dietitian.

- Maintain a regular eating schedule. Your body needs it.

- Lose weight if you carry extra pounds.

- Exercise. It lowers blood sugar and, combined with weight loss, can make the disease easier to manage.

- See your eye doctor at least once a year. Diabetes is the leading cause of blindness.

- Don't despair. Seek emotional support from friends and family, or call a counselor if necessary.

- Eat foods with a low glycemic index (such as beans, nuts, and dairy products), as they release sugar slowly into the bloodstream.

Diarrhea
RIDING OUT THE RUNS

It's got all kinds of colorful nicknames, including "Greased Lightning," "Turkey Trots," and "Montezuma's Revenge." Your 11-year-old may even sing a little ditty about it. Just saying the word diarrhea gets a reaction from most people—they either giggle or turn pale. Diarrhea is probably one of the most unpleasant problems that plagues us. And it's a common malady. Americans usually suffer from diarrhea a couple times a year. For most adults, diarrhea isn't serious. And it does give you a chance to ponder some redecorating ideas for the bathroom.

The Rundown on Diarrhea

On a typical day, you eat a hoagie and drink an iced tea and your meal makes its way through your digestive system without any problems. By the time it reaches the intestines, your food is mostly fluid with bits of solid material. The intestines reabsorb most of the fluid, and the solid stuff is excreted in the usual fashion. But when you've got diarrhea, something blocks the intestine's ability to absorb fluid. You've got loads of watery fluids mixed in with your stool, and you get that "gotta go" feeling.

WHEN TO CALL THE DOCTOR

Most diarrhea has to run its course. However, diarrhea can be a sign of a more serious problem. If you're concerned, here are some symptoms that warrant a trip to the emergency room or a call to your family physician.

- Your diarrhea symptoms last more than 48 hours
- You have severe stomach cramps
- You have blood or pus in your stool
- You start showing any signs of severe dehydration such as dizziness when you stand, urinating less frequently or in very small amounts, dark yellow urine, increased thirst, and dry skin
- You have fever or chills

There are essentially two types of diarrhea: acute and chronic. Thankfully, the vast majority of diarrhea is acute, or short term. This type of diarrhea keeps you on the toilet for a couple of days but doesn't stick around long. Acute diarrhea is also known as non-inflammatory diarrhea. Its symptoms are what most people associate with the condition: frequent, watery stools accompanied by stomach cramps, gas, and nausea.

Acute diarrhea usually has a bacterial or viral culprit. Gastroenteritis, mistakenly called the "stomach flu," is one of the most common infections that cause diarrhea. Gastroenteritis can be caused by many different viruses. Eating or drinking foods contaminated with bacteria can also cause diarrhea. Other causes of acute diarrhea are lactose intolerance, sweeteners such as sorbitol, over-the-counter antacids that contain magnesium, too much vitamin C, and some antibiotics.

If you have chronic, or long-term, diarrhea that comes on suddenly and stays for weeks, you may have a more serious condition such as irritable bowel syndrome or a severe food allergy.

Dehydration Dangers

With any kind of diarrhea you lose a lot of fluids. One of the quickest ways you can end up going from the bathroom to the emergency room is to take a pass on liquids while you're sick. Fluids not only keep things running smoothly in your body, they also keep electrolyte levels balanced. Electrolytes are sodium, potassium, and chloride salts that your body needs for proper organ function. An electrolyte imbalance can make your heart beat irregularly, causing life-threatening problems. Though drinking or eating anything while you're running back and forth to the bathroom might sound grotesque, it will help make you more comfortable and get you back on your feet more quickly.

Though experts don't see eye to eye on what fluids are best during a bout with diarrhea, they do agree that getting two to three quarts of fluid a day is a good idea. When you drink, it's easier on the tummy if you sip instead of gulp (who has the energy for gulping?) and if you drink cool, not cold or hot, fluids. Here are some tried-and-true fluids that should get you through the rough days.

• Decaffeinated tea with a little sugar

• Sports drinks

• Bouillon

• Chicken broth

• Orange juice

Though it may not sound logical to put diarrhea and food in the same sentence, if you don't put something in your body while you're enduring tummy troubles, you might end up getting sicker. There are loads of good things from the kitchen that will ease your grumbling stomach, and there are a few things that will prevent those diarrhea-causing agents from coming back for a return engagement.

FROM THE CUPBOARD

BLUEBERRIES. Blueberry root is a long-time folk remedy for diarrhea. In Sweden, doctors prescribe a soup made with dried blueberries for tummy problems. Blueberries are rich in anthocyanosides, which have antioxidant and antibacterial properties, as well as tannins, which combat diarrhea.

CHAMOMILE TEA. Chamomile is good for treating intestinal inflammation, and it has antispasmodic properties as well. Brew yourself a cup of chamomile tea from packaged tea bags or buy chamomile flowers and steep 1 teaspoon of them and 1 teaspoon of peppermint leaves in a cup of boiling water for 15 minutes. Drink 3 cups a day.

COOKED CEREALS. Starchy foods, such as precooked rice or tapioca cereals, can help ease your tummy. Prepare the cereal according to the directions on the box, making it as thick as you can stomach it. Just avoid adding too much sugar or salt, as these can aggravate diarrhea. It's probably a good idea to avoid oatmeal since it's high in fiber and your intestines can't tolerate the added bulk during a bout with diarrhea.

POTATOES. This is another starchy food that can help restore nutrients and comfort your stomach. But eating french fries won't help. Fried foods tend to aggravate an aching tummy. Other root vegetables such as carrots (cooked, of course) are also easy on an upset stomach, and they are loaded with nutrients.

RICE. Cooked white rice is another starchy food that can be handled by someone recovering from diarrhea.

SUGAR. To make your own fluid replacement, mix 4 teaspoons sugar and ½ teaspoon salt with 1 quart water. Mixing electrolytes (such as salt) with a form of glucose (sugar) helps the body to better absorb the nutrients.

FROM THE FRUIT BASKET

BANANA. Long known as a soother for tummy trouble, this potassium-rich fruit can restore nutrients and is easy to digest.

ORANGE PEEL. Orange peel tea is a folk remedy that is believed to aid in digestion. Place a chopped orange peel

FOODS TO AVOID WHEN YOU'VE GOT TUMMY TROUBLE

- Caffeine. It stimulates the nervous system, including the intestines.
- Sweeteners such as sorbitol, xylitol, and mannitol. These are mostly found in fruit juices and sugarless candy.
- Milk and cheese. The intestines work extra hard to digest the enzymes in these dairy products. While your body is down for the count, and even a few days after you're better, you might want to avoid dairy of any kind except for yogurt.
- Fiber. Now is not the time to bulk up. Fiber is simply too hard for an aching tummy to digest.
- Sugar. Some sugar is good during a case of diarrhea—it can help you absorb electrolytes needed for rehydration—but too much can make things worse.

(preferably from an organic orange, as peels otherwise may contain pesticides and dyes) into a pot and cover with 1 pint boiling water. Let it stand until the water is cooled. You can sweeten it with a little sugar or honey.

FROM THE REFRIGERATOR

YOGURT. Look for yogurt with live cultures. These "cultures" are friendly bacteria that can go in and line your intestines, providing you protection from the bad guys. If you've already got diarrhea, yogurt can help produce lactic acid in your intestines, which can kill off the nasty bacteria and get you feeling better, faster.

FROM THE SPICE RACK

FENUGREEK SEEDS. Science has given the nod to this folk remedy. But this one is for adults only. Mix ½ teaspoon fenugreek seeds with water and drink up.

MORE DO'S AND DON'TS

- To ease stomach pain, try resting with a heating pad on your belly.

- Don't take antidiarrheal medications at the onset of your illness. Let your body rid itself of whatever's causing the problem first.

- Wash your hands thoroughly and frequently, especially before preparing food. You don't want to pass your illness to everyone in the household.

Diverticular Disease
PREVENTING PROBLEMS

Diverticulosis is a common condition in which small pouches, called diverticula, develop in the colon. It happens when the inner lining of the large intestine is forced, under pressure, through weak spots in the outer layer of the colon. No one is sure what causes diverticulosis, but a low-fiber diet and lack of exercise have been shown to put you at greater risk. The diverticular pouches are present in about 50 percent of people over age 60, and they themselves are not much of a problem. However, when a food particle or piece of waste material lodges in a pouch, it can become inflamed and cause a more serious illness called diverticulitis. Diverticulitis can range from a mild infection to a severe one requiring hospitalization and even surgery.

Symptoms

Diverticulosis usually causes no symptoms. Most people won't even know they have the condition unless it has shown up on a routine colonoscopy or developed into diverticulitis. But diverticulitis does have symptoms, including the following:

WHEN TO CALL THE DOCTOR

- If you experience severe abdominal pain along with fever, swelling, chills, and nausea or vomiting, go to the emergency room immediately. Your symptoms can't wait for a call to the doctor.
- If there's blood in the stool or your stool is black and tarlike. You may be bleeding internally.
- If pain persists in spite of treatment

- Abdominal cramping, usually more severe on the lower-left side
- Abdominal pain triggered by touch
- Nausea
- Gas, belching, bloating
- Fever
- Diarrhea, constipation, or very thin stools
- Blood in the stools
- General feeling of being tired or run-down

If you have any of these symptoms, don't try to self-diagnose. Call a doctor or, if the symptoms are severe, get yourself to the doctor's office or a hospital emergency room. Diverticulitis that's untreated can lead to perforation of the colon, formation of an abscess, or peritonitis, a life-threatening infection of the lining of the abdominal cavity.

Diverticula don't go away. Once you have them, you're stuck with them. It's a good idea to adjust your lifestyle to avoid flare-ups, and for mild symptoms there's relief to be found in the kitchen.

Warning! The following are to help prevent the development of diverticulitis or to ease the mildest of symptoms. For all other symptoms, see a doctor!

FROM THE CUPBOARD

BARLEY. This grain is a digestive anti-inflammatory. Add some to vegetable soup or stew. Or buy some barley flour, flakes, and grits, and use them in your cooking.

BROWN RICE. It's easy on the digestive system and rich in fiber, and it calms inflammation and spasms in the colon. Eat it plain or as a dessert with a little honey, mix it with vegetables for a stir-fry, try it in the morning as a breakfast food instead of oatmeal, or boil it for a tea and drink the liquid in addition to eating the rice. There are no limits to the ways you can serve up brown rice.

GARLIC. This can help prevent infection. Eat 1 clove, three times a day. Chop it into a salad or add it to soup or stew. Red pasta sauces, however, are not good choices since tomato-based, spicy, and acidic foods can exacerbate symptoms.

FABULOUS FIBER (A.K.A. BULK)

Fiber, also known as bulk, is essential to alleviating problems associated with diverticulitis and for having a healthy colon. Everyone needs 25 to 30 grams a day. The problem is, even though we think we're getting plenty of fiber, most of us are getting only half of what we need.

Remember, though, to add fiber to your diet slowly at first. Try a little one day, skip a day, then add a little more the next. Too much too soon can lead to constipation. And be sure to drink plenty of water as you're adding fiber—at least 8 glasses a day. That helps push all that added fiber on through the digestive system. The faster it's gone, the less it, or any other foods, will get lodged in one of the diverticula and cause a problem.

FACTS ABOUT DIVERTICULOSIS

- 10 percent of people over age 40 have diverticulosis
- 50 percent over age 60 have diverticulosis
- Almost everyone over age 80 has diverticulosis
- About 20 percent of those with diverticulosis will develop diverticulitis

FROM THE REFRIGERATOR

PAPAYA. This soothes diverticulitis. Find a nice, ripe, red-tinged papaya, cut it open, toss away the seeds, and eat. Use it in a fruit salad; it's especially good with melons. Or put it in the blender and make juice. Add a little honey to sweeten it up, if necessary. Papaya has an unusual but enjoyable flavor.

PEAR. Another fruit that can soothe inflammation, pears don't need any doctoring to eat. Simply find one that's ripe and enjoy.

POTATOES. They're tasty and nourishing, and they have soothing, anti-inflammatory properties that are especially good for digestive woes. Because grease can aggravate diverticulitis, avoid fried potatoes of any sort. But any other cooking method will do: baking, broiling, or boiling.

MORE DO'S & DON'TS

- Exercise. Everything in your body works better, including your digestive tract, when you exercise regularly.

- Skip the caffeine. It can cause digestive upset.

- Don't rush things. It takes time for your bowels to move, so allow sufficient time.

- Cut back on red meats. They weaken the wall of the colon, which is where the pouches of diverticulosis start.

Fever

FEELING THE HEAT

Fever is a good thing. It's your body's attempt to kill off invading bacteria and other nasty organisms that can't survive the heat. The hypothalamus, which is the body's thermostat, senses the assault on the body and turns up the heat much the way you turn up the thermostat when you feel cold. It's a simple defense mechanism, and the sweat that comes with a fever is merely a way to cool the body down.

It used to be standard medical practice to knock that fever out as quickly as possible. Not so anymore. The value of fever is recognized, and since a fever will usually subside when the infection that's causing it runs its course, modern thinking is to ride out that fever, especially if it stays under 102°F in adults. However, if a fever is making you uncomfortable or interfering with your ability to eat, drink, or sleep, treat it. Your body needs adequate nutrition, hydration, and rest to fight the underlying cause of the fever.

Fever is a symptom, not an illness, and so there's no specific cure. But there are some fever-relievers in the kitchen that may make you feel better for the duration.

WHEN TO CALL THE DOCTOR

- In infants under 3 months, 100°F or above
- Infants 3 to 6 months, 101°F or above
- In children and adults under 60, 104°F
- In adults over 60, 102°F
- In adults and children, 101°F for more than three days
- In children, if febrile seizures develop
- If pain, diarrhea, swollen joints, rash, or stiff neck occur with fever

Be aware that the most significant side effect of fever is dehydration. Drink lots of fluids to help prevent dehydration.

FROM THE CUPBOARD

CREAM OF TARTAR. Try this fever tea. Combine 1½ teaspoons cream of tartar, ½ teaspoon lemon juice, 2½ cups warm water, and ½ teaspoon honey. Drink 4 to 6 ounces at a time.

PINEAPPLE. Fresh is best. It's one of nature's anti-inflammatory agents, which can help ease the discomfort of a fever. Pineapple is also packed with juice that can prevent dehydration.

RAISINS. Put ¾ cup chopped raisins in 7½ cups water. Bring to a boil, then simmer until the water has been reduced by one-third. Drink a little of this several times a day to keep yourself hydrated during a fever.

SALT. An Ayurvedic remedy for fever is to mix 1 teaspoon salt into a bowl of cool water. Take two clean dishtowels, dip them in the water, then place one on the forehead and one over the belly button.

FROM THE FREEZER

POPSICLE. These can reduce the risk of dehydration. Fruit juice bars are good, too.

FROM THE REFRIGERATOR

APPLE WATER. It tastes good, relieves the miseries of fever, and keeps the body hydrated. To make it, peel, skin, core, and slice 3 sweet apples. Put them in a pan with 3¾ cups water. Bring to a boil, then simmer until the apples are barely mushy. Remove, strain without pressing apple puree into the liquid, and add 2 tablespoons honey. Drink and enjoy.

BLACKBERRY VINEGAR. This is a great fever elixir, but it takes several days to prepare. Pour cider vinegar over a pound or two of blackberries, then cover the container and store it in a cool, dark place for three days. Strain for a day, since it takes time for all the liquid to drain from the berries, and collect the liquid in another container. Then add 2 cups sugar to each 2½ cups juice. Bring to a boil, then simmer for 5 minutes while you skim the scum off the top. Cool and store in an airtight jar in a cool place. Mix 1 teaspoonful with water to quench the thirst caused by a fever.

CILANTRO (CORIANDER LEAVES). Nice, fresh cilantro can be turned into a simple fever remedy. Wash thoroughly and place a handful of leaves in a blender with ⅓ cup water. Blend thoroughly, then strain, reserving the liquid. Take 2 teaspoons of the liquid three times a day.

FRUIT JUICE. It will replace the fluids lost through sweating. Lemonade is a good choice, too.

GINGER. This can help break a high fever. Grate 2 tablespoons fresh ginger and add to 2 cups boiling water.

FASCINATING FACT
Shivering increases the amount of heat your body produces by up to five times.

HERBS THAT'LL MAKE YOU SWEAT

Many traditional folk fever remedies are called diaphoretics, meaning they'll make you sweat. Properties in the following diaphoretic herbs increase blood circulation to the skin, which brings on the sweat. And that's a good thing because sweating cools the body during a fever. Take any of the following herbs as hot teas: agueweed, boneset, bupleurum, catnip, dandelion root and leaves, elderberries and flowers, feverfew, ginseng, strawberry leaf, and yarrow. Just be sure to drink plenty of water, because sweating can cause dehydration. Then go to bed and get some rest.

Steep 30 minutes. Add a little honey to sweeten, and drink a cup of the warm beverage every two to three hours.

LETTUCE. Pour a pint of boiling water over an entire head of lettuce and let it steep, covered, for 15 minutes. Strain, sweeten the liquid to taste, and drink. In addition to keeping you hydrated, this lettuce infusion may help you sleep better.

FROM THE SINK

WATER. Drink lots of it to prevent dehydration. Sponging the body with lukewarm water can relieve fever symptoms, but it's recommended that you use fever-reducing medication first to reduce the possibility of chills and shivering. Do not use cold water or ice on the body.

FROM THE SPICE RACK

BASIL. Mix 1 teaspoon basil with ¼ teaspoon black pepper. Steep in 1 cup hot water to make a tea. Add 1 teaspoon honey. Drink two to three times a day.

OREGANO. A tea made from a mixture of some spice rack staples can help reduce fever. Steep 1 teaspoon each of oregano and marjoram in a pint of boiling water for 30 minutes. Strain, and drink warm a couple times a day. Refrigerate unused portion until needed, then gently warm.

SAGE. Mix 2 teaspoons dried sage with 1 teaspoon dried peppermint. Pour 1 cup boiling water over these and steep 15 minutes. Strain and sweeten with honey. Drink 2 to 3 cups per day, rewarmed. Add a little honey to sweeten the taste.

MORE DO'S & DON'TS

- Do not sponge alcohol on the body to reduce fever. It can cause chills and increased fever.

- Use analgesics if necessary. Acetaminophen will reduce a fever, as will aspirin. However, NEVER give aspirin to children under 18 without first consulting the doctor. The result can be Reye's syndrome, a potentially fatal disease.

- Skip the alcohol and caffeine. They're diuretics, and you don't need to lose more fluid.

- Use only light clothing and blankets. Cover up just enough to be comfortable and keep from shivering. Heavy clothing and blankets will only make the fever go higher.

- If you don't feel like eating, don't. Just make sure you get sufficient fluids. Do reintroduce yourself to foods gradually, though, if you haven't been eating very much.

Flu (Influenza)

SURVIVING THE SIEGE

Boo hoo if you've got the flu. Unlike the common cold, which causes a stuffy nose, sore throat, and sneezing, the flu is a viral infection that strikes the entire body with a vengeance. The  misery starts suddenly with chills and fever and spirals into more unpleasant symptoms that will take you out of commission: a sore throat, dry cough, stuffy or runny nose, headache, nausea, vomiting, severe muscle aches and pains, weakness, backache, and loss of appetite. Some people even experience pain and stiffness in the joints.

The worst of your symptoms will last about three to five days, but others, such as cough and fatigue, can linger for weeks. And a bout with the flu can deliver a double whammy if you develop a secondary infection, such as an ear or sinus infection or bronchitis. Even pneumonia can be a complication—and a potentially serious one—of influenza.

Flu viruses strike like clockwork in the United States. Every year they begin to show up in October and exit in April. Peak flu season is December and January.

Flu is a highly contagious illness, spread by droplets

from the respiratory tract of an infected person. These can be airborne, such as those released after a person coughs or sneezes, or they can be transferred via an infected person's hands.

Taking a yearly flu shot can help you ward off infection, and these are particularly recommended for senior citizens, people with compromised immune systems, or people with asthma. They won't give you 100 percent protection, but they will significantly increase your chances of avoiding it.

If you do get the flu, there are kitchen remedies to help ease your suffering.

WHEN TO CALL THE DOCTOR

- If flu symptoms are accompanied by a high fever that lasts more than three days
- If a cough persists, becomes worse, or is associated with chest pains and shortness of breath
- If the flu drags on and you don't get better
- If you have lung or heart disease, consult your physician at the first sign of flu. The elderly and the very young should also be taken to a doctor at the first sign of flu.

FROM THE CUPBOARD

BROTH. Canned broth, whether it's beef, chicken, or vegetable, will keep you hydrated and help liquefy any mucous secretions. Broth is easy to keep down, even when you have no appetite, and it will provide at least some nutrients.

HONEY. A hacking cough can keep you and every other household member up all night. Keep the peace with honey. Honey has long been used in traditional Chinese medicine for coughs. It's a simple enough recipe: Mix 1 tablespoon honey into 1 cup hot water, stir well, and enjoy. Honey acts as a natural expectorant, promoting the flow of mucus. Squeeze some lemon in if you want a little tartness.

MUSTARD. Not to discredit dear old Grandma, but she didn't come up with the mustard plaster, although by the way she touts its virtues, you might believe so. Actually, this ancient remedy for the flu, chest colds, and bronchitis dates back to the ancient Romans, who early on understood the healing properties of mustard. Mustard is loaded with antimicrobial and anti-inflammatory properties, many of which can be inhaled through the vapors.

Impress Grandma by making a mustard plaster with 1 tablespoon dry mustard and 2 to 4 tablespoons flour. Mix both with 1 egg white (optional) and warm water to form a paste. Next, find a clean handkerchief or square of muslin large enough to cover the upper chest. Smear the cloth the same way you'd smear mustard on a sandwich, then plop another cloth over it. Dab olive oil on the patient's skin and apply the mustard plaster to the upper chest. Check the skin every few minutes since a mustard plaster can burn. Remove after a few minutes. Afterward, wash off any traces of mustard from the skin.

TEA. A cup of hot tea is just another way to take your fluids, which are so essential when you have the flu. Just be sure to choose decaffeinated varieties. Caffeine is a mild diuretic, which is counterproductive when you have the flu, and you certainly don't want to be awakened with the need to use the bathroom when you need your rest!

FROM THE REFRIGERATOR

JUICE. Any flavor or kind will do. Just drink lots of juice both to keep yourself hydrated and to give yourself some extra vitamins.

LEMON. The lovely lemon may cause a puckered face if eaten raw, but in a hot beverage lemons will have you smiling. Hot lemonade has been used as a flu remedy since Roman times and is still highly regarded in the folk traditions of New England. Lemons, being highly acidic, help make mucous membranes distasteful to bacteria and viruses. Lemon oil, which gives the juice its fragrance, is like a wonder drug containing antibacterial, antiviral, antifungal, and anti-inflammatory constituents. The oil also acts as an expectorant. To make this flu-fighting fruit drink, place 1 chopped lemon—skin, pulp, and all—into 1 cup boiling water. While the lemon steeps for five minutes, inhale the steam. Strain, add honey (to taste), and enjoy. Drink hot lemonade three to four times a day throughout your illness.

FROM THE SPICE RACK

PEPPER. Pepper is an irritant (try sniffing some), yet this annoying characteristic is a plus for those suffering from coughs with thick mucus. The irritating property of pepper stimulates circulation and the flow of mucus. Place 1 teaspoon black pepper into a cup and sweeten things up with the addition of 1 tablespoon honey. Fill with boiling water, let steep for 10 to 15 minutes, stir, and sip.

MYTHS ABOUT THE DREADED FLU

Myth #1: The 24-hour flu.

Fact: There is no such thing as a 24-hour flu, although we wish it were so. The sudden onslaught of vomiting, diarrhea, and a general feeling of malaise that is intense for a few hours, but subsides after 24 hours, is indeed caused by a viral agent, but not the one that causes influenza. The correct term should be "the 24-hour attack of gastroenteritis," which is an infection that affects the gastrointestinal tract.

Myth #2: Going outside without a hat or catching a chill causes the flu.

Fact: Venturing outside ill-prepared for the elements may not be the brightest idea, but it doesn't directly cause the flu. Several scientific studies have shown that people exposed to cold temperatures for several hours fare no worse than those kept toasty warm. This myth grows from the observation that a severe chill is one of the first flu symptoms. Thus, people conclude that being chilled leads to the flu.

THYME. It's time to try thyme when the mucous membranes are stuffed, the head aches, and the body is hot with fever. Wonderfully fragrant, thyme delights the senses (if you can smell when sick) and works as a powerful expectorant and antiseptic, thanks to its constituent oil, thymol. By cupping your hands around a mug of thyme tea and breathing in the steam, the thymol sets to work through your upper respiratory tract, loosening mucus and inhibiting bacteria from settling down to stay. Make thyme tea in a snap by adding 1 teaspoon dried thyme leaves to 1 cup boiling water. Let steep for five minutes while inhaling the steam. Strain the tea, sweeten with honey (to taste), and slowly sip.

MORE DO'S AND DON'TS

- Get plenty of rest. Okay, you may not need to be told this, at least when the flu first hits. But rest is essential to allow your body to fight the virus. So indulge yourself, you've got a good reason to.

- Drink lots of fluids. Water's good, as are teas, juice, and soups. Off-limits are coffee and soda pop, as they may contain caffeine and have no nutritional benefits whatsoever.

- If you have lots of aches and pains and just can't get comfortable, use an over-the-counter pain reliever. But don't give aspirin to anyone under age 18 because of the risk of Reye's syndrome, a potentially fatal illness that is linked with aspirin use and the flu in young people.

Gallbladder Problems
Averting an Attack

Unless you've had prob-
lems with your gallbladder,
you probably don't know
much about it. Be thankful. If you
do know the specifics of your gallbladder, you're probably one of the
10 to 15 percent of Americans who
have gallstones. While half of those
with gallstones experience no
symptoms, the other half can have chronic problems,
including discomfort and pain in the upper abdomen,
indigestion, nausea, and intolerance of fatty foods. A gallbladder attack, which occurs when a gallstone gets stuck
in the bile duct, can double you over in pain for hours
and leave you wishing something, anything, could make
you feel better.

Casting Stones

The gallbladder is a little pear-shaped pouch tucked
behind the lobes of the liver. Its main job is to store up the
cholesterol-rich bile that's secreted by the liver. Bile helps
your body digest fatty foods. So when that piece of prime
rib reaches the intestines, it sends a message up to the
gallbladder to send some bile their way. Once the bile
saturates your steak, it becomes more digestible and easily

makes its way through the rest of the digestive process.

At least that's the way things should work. But the reality is that many people, especially older people and women, will have some gallbladder trouble. Ninety percent of the time that trouble is in the form of gallstones. Gallstones form when the bile contains excessive amounts of cholesterol. When there isn't enough bile to saturate the cholesterol, the cholesterol begins to crystallize, and you get a gallstone. These tough bits can be as tiny as a grain of sand or as large as a golf ball. You may not even know you have gallstones unless you happen to have an ultrasound or X ray of your tummy. But the 20 percent of the time that gallstones do cause problems, it's excruciatingly painful.

> **WHEN TO CALL THE DOCTOR**
> - If you have a fever
> - If your skin or eyes have a yellowish tinge
> - If you have persistent pain
> - If you are sweating
> - If you have chills
> - If you have clay-colored stools

Gallstones become a problem when they get pushed out of the gallbladder and into the tube that connects the liver and the small intestine. The tube gets blocked, and you get 20 minutes to 4 hours of indescribable agony. Pain usually radiates from your upper right abdominal area to your lower right chest, and it can even leave your shoulder and back in agony. Gallstones typically fall back into the gallbladder or make their way through the duct, leaving you feeling better. After you have an attack, you'll

SURVIVING WITHOUT A GALLBLADDER

Believe it or not, you actually can get along just fine without your gallbladder. Instead of being stored in the gallbladder, bile flows directly from the liver into the small intestine. Diarrhea may be a side effect, and you may have higher blood cholesterol levels. You may also risk stomach upset if you eat too much fat at one time. But aside from that, life will continue as normal—that is, minus the chronic pain from gallbladder attacks.

probably be sore and wonder what in the world happened.

Sometimes, though, the gallstones can get stuck in the bile duct. Symptoms of a stuck gallstone include chills, vomiting, and possibly jaundice in addition to the pain described above.

Who's at Risk?

Pregnancy, obesity, diabetes, liver disease, a sedentary lifestyle, a high fat diet, and certain forms of anemia can all increase the risk of gallstones. People who are overweight and lose and gain weight repeatedly are more susceptible to gallstones, as are women who have had two or more children. Lack of exercise is a significant contributor to the development of gallstones. In fact, according to the Nurses' Health Study, inactivity can actually account for more than half of the risk of developing gallstones. Women are twice as likely as men to develop gallstones, although the reasons are unclear. And people older than 60 years of age have a greater risk of gallstones.

Other risk factors include a family history of gallstones and taking hormones, such as birth control pills or estrogen.

Take heart. There are some specific things you can find in your kitchen to help you avoid a gallstone attack and even prevent gallstones from forming in the first place. What you eat has a great effect on whether or not you develop gallstones. And research is finding that certain

foods can help you avert a painful attack or, better yet, avoid gallstones altogether.

FROM THE CUPBOARD

COFFEE. New studies are finding that drinking a couple of cups of java a day can prevent gallstones. One study discovered that men who drank 2 to 3 cups of regular coffee a day cut their risk of developing gallstones by 40 percent. Four cups a day reduced the risk by 45 percent. Researchers are not sure what it is about coffee that helps reduce the risk of forming gallstones, but the effect was the same whether the coffee consumed was cheap, store-bought instant coffee or high-priced espresso. It might be the caffeine; however, teas and soft drinks containing caffeine did not produce the same effect—and neither did decaffeinated coffee.

HIGH-FIBER CEREAL. People who eat a sugary, high-fat diet probably will have more problems with their gallstones. But adding in some fiber-rich foods and avoiding the sugary snacks and fatty foods can help you keep your gallbladder healthy. Grabbing some cereal in the morning will also get something in your tummy. Studies have shown that going for long periods without eating, such as skipping breakfast, can make you more prone to getting a gallstone.

LENTILS. An interesting study found that women who ate loads of lentils, nuts, beans, peas, lima beans, and oranges were more resistant to gallbladder attacks than women who didn't eat much of the stuff.

FROM THE REFRIGERATOR

RED BELL PEPPER. Getting loads of vitamin C in your diet can help you avoid gallstones, and one red bell pepper has 95 mg of the helpful vitamin—more than the 60 mg a day the government recommends for men and women over age 15. A recent study found that people who had more vitamin C in their blood were less likely to get the painful stones.

SALMON. Research is finding that omega-3 fatty acids, found in fatty fish such as salmon, may help prevent gallstones.

VEGETABLES. Eating your veggies is a good way to ward off gallstones. One study found that vegetarian women were only half as likely to have gallstones as their carnivorous counterparts. Researchers aren't exactly sure how vegetables counteract gallstones, but they believe vegetables help reduce the amount of cholesterol in bile.

WINE. Half a glass of wine a day can avert gallstone attacks. Scientists discovered that drinking half a glass of wine or beer cut the number of gallstone attacks by 40 percent. But don't go overboard. The study didn't find that drinking more than half a glass would offer any more protection.

MORE DO'S AND DON'TS

• Exercise! Staying active can cut your risk of developing gallstones in half.

- Lose some weight. Being overweight, even as little as 10 pounds, can double your risk of getting gallstones.

- Diet sensibly. If you are overweight, plan on shedding pounds slowly. Losing weight too fast can increase your chances of developing gallstones.

- Reduce your saturated fat intake. Too much fat in the diet increases your risk of gallstones. But don't cut back too drastically. You need some fat to give the gallbladder the message to empty bile. If you're trying to lose weight, don't go below 20 percent calories from fat.

- Eat a low fat, low-cholesterol, high-fiber diet. Multiple studies show this is your best bet for a healthy body and a healthy gallbladder.

SHOCKING THOSE STONES: THE WAVE OF THE FUTURE

Until recently, most people who had recurring painful bouts with gallstones had one choice—get rid of the gallbladder. But there's a new procedure that may allow people to get rid of their gallstones without losing any body parts. The procedure is based on the same shock-wave theory that uses high-frequency sound waves to demolish kidney stones. But this is an invasive procedure. The doctor inserts a tube into the gallbladder via a small puncture hole, and the shock is delivered directly to the gallstones. Then the fragments of the stones are scooped up and removed from the body. The whole process takes about an hour and leaves you on R & R for a few days. But compared to the major surgery required to remove your gallbladder, this procedure is a breeze.

Headaches
THWARTING THE THROBBING

The day starts with screaming kids, continues slowly onward with stop 'n' go traffic, and ends on a sour note with an angry boss. By this point, you are ready to chop your head off in order to relieve the pounding pain.

You can take a little comfort in knowing that almost everyone has had such a day...and such a headache. Yet some people fare worse than others do. An estimated 45 million Americans get chronic, recurring headaches, while as many as 18 million of those suffer from painful, debilitating migraines.

The Three Kinds of Headaches

Although there are nearly two dozen types of headaches, they all fall into three basic categories: tension, vascular, and organic.

Tension headaches, the most common of the trio, cause a dull, nonthrobbing pain, usually accompanied by tightness in the scalp or neck. Triggers range from depression to everyday stresses such as screaming kids and traffic jams.

Vascular headaches are more intense, severe, throbbing, and piercing: They take first prize for pain. Cluster and migraine headaches fall into this category. Triggers for cluster headaches are unknown, although excessive smoking and alcohol consumption can ignite them. Migraines are thought to be caused by heredity, diet, stress, menstruation, and environmental factors such as cigarette smoke.

Less common are organic headaches, in which pain becomes increasingly worse and is accompanied by other symptoms, such as vomiting, coordination problems, visual disturbances, or speech or personality changes. Triggers include tumors, infections, or diseases of the brain, eyes, ears, and nose.

If you are prone to the usual tension headache, head to the kitchen for a variety of remedies that can help your throbbing head.

FROM THE FREEZER

ICE. A washcloth dipped in ice-cold water and placed over the pain site is an easy way to relieve a headache. An ice

WHEN TO CALL THE DOCTOR

- If you get daily headaches
- If you get headaches after intense coughing or sneezing
- If you have pain in the ear or eyes
- If you experience nausea or vomiting
- If you experience vision changes
- If you have hallucinations
- If you experience sensitivity to light and sound
- If you have weakness or dizziness
- If you lose consciousness
- If you have a severe, debilitating headache

compress works well, too. Place a handful of crushed ice cubes into a zipper-type plastic bag (a bag of frozen vegetables is a good substitute), and cover it with a dry washcloth. Apply where needed. Whatever method you use, try to apply the cold compress as soon as possible after the headache develops. Relief typically starts within 20 minutes of use.

FROM THE REFRIGERATOR

PEACH JUICE. Drinking peach juice or apricot nectar can help alleviate the nausea that sometimes accompanies a bad headache.

FROM THE SINK

HOT WATER. If snow is falling and the last thing you want on your head is an ice pack, turn to heat for soothing relief. Dip a washcloth into hot but not scalding water. Squeeze out and apply over your eyes or on the pain site. Leave the compress on for 30 minutes, rewarming as necessary.

FROM THE SPICE RACK

PEPPERMINT. A dab of peppermint oil rubbed on the temples can ease a tension headache. Don't try this with children or if you have sensitive skin, as the oil can have a burning effect.

CLOVES AND OTHER SPICES. Here's a remedy that includes the whole kitchen sink...or should we say the whole spice rack? A blend of scented herbs eases away tension headaches. Look into your spice rack. Do you have dried marjoram, rosemary, and mint? They work well together. And if you have dried lavender and rose petals, they make

HERBAL REMEDY

If you suffer from recurring headaches, you might want to plant a little feverfew in your herb garden (or grow the herb in a windowsill pot). This lovely, easy-to-nurture herb has long been used as a headache remedy, especially for migraines. Feverfew causes blood vessels to dilate and inhibits the secretion of substances that cause pain and inflammation (such as histamine and serotonin) through the substance parthenolide.

You have two choices when it comes to taking feverfew: eating it raw or drinking it in a tea. If you prefer the au naturel way, chew on 2 to 3 of the bitter-tasting leaves each time you have a headache. (Don't exceed 4 leaves a day.) Feverfew may cause mouth irritation. Should this occur, place a leaf in a salad or sandwich. To make a tea, place 1 tablespoon dried feverfew into 1 cup boiling water. Steep for ten minutes, strain, and sip the tea for relief.

wonderful additions to the mix. Put 4 tablespoons of each (or whichever you have) into a cloth sachet bag. Add 1 tablespoon cloves. Close up the sachet bag, and whenever you have a headache or feel one coming on, hold the bag to your nose and inhale deeply until you feel it subsiding. (If you don't have a sachet bag, a clean handkerchief tied around the herbs works fine.) You can also apply this bundle of herbs to your head when you rest.

ROSEMARY. Rosemary is a well-recognized folk cure for easing pain in the United States, China, and Europe. One of its constituents, rosmarinic acid, is an anti-inflammatory similar to aspirin and ibuprofen. Since rosmarinic acid is also an important constituent in sage, the two herbs are often combined to make a pain-relieving tea. Place 1 teaspoon crushed rosemary leaves and 1 teaspoon

PLEASURE AND PAIN

Ice cream, that summertime delight, can truly make you scream—or at least writhe in agony. Eating ice cream can cause an ice-cream headache, and anyone who has eaten an icy treat too fast knows the pain well. What sparks this headache is a change in mouth temperature. As the icy dessert touches the top of your mouth (or back of your throat), it causes a nerve reaction that swells blood vessels in the head. The result: an intense, shooting pain that lasts for 30 to 60 seconds. The cure: Spend more time licking your ice cream cone and less time gulping it down—and keep icy cold foods to the side of your mouth.

crushed sage leaves in a cup. Fill with boiling water. Cover to prevent the volatile oils from escaping, and steep until the tea reaches room temperature. Take ½-cup doses two to three times a day. You don't have to mix the two herbs to benefit from rosmarinic acid, however. If you only have one, make a tea of it alone.

MORE DO'S AND DON'TS

• Lie down. Sometimes the best headache treatment is to go to bed and sleep. For some headaches, sleep interrupts the pain cycle.

• Keep it dark. Bright light, whether it's sunlight or the glare of a computer screen, can bring on a headache or make one you already have worse. If you're sensitive to light, wear sunglasses outdoors and adjust your blinds so that intense light doesn't hit your eyes. If you've already got a headache, darken the room where you're resting.

- Distract yourself from stress. Try to concentrate on pleasant thoughts only, and shut out tension-producing ones. Stress can bring on a headache or make one you already have much worse.

- Check for tension. Many people unconsciously clench their jaw muscles, grip the steering wheel tightly, furrow their brows, or make fists when they're tense. All of these can lead to a headache. If you notice you're in the grip of tension, force yourself to breathe slowly and deeply, and gently relax your tense muscles.

- Don't smoke. Aside from the fact that it's unhealthy, smoking can give you a headache or make one worse.

Heartburn
PUTTING OUT THE FIRE

Boy, oh boy, did you do it this time. You added that heaping second helping to all the platter pickings you couldn't resist, and what do you have? Indigestion (an incomplete or imperfect digestion), that's what. And it may be accompanied by pain, nausea, vomiting, heartburn, gas, and belching. All this because you couldn't resist temptation. Well, don't worry. It happens to everybody, and it goes away.

So, now that you've eaten until you're about ready to burst, what's next? The couch, maybe? Stretch out, let your digestive system do its thing, take a nap?

Wrong! The worst thing you can do after a binge is to lie down. That can cause heartburn, also known as acid indigestion. It's the feeling you get when digestive acid escapes your stomach and irritates the esophagus, the tube that leads from your throat to your stomach. After you eat, heartburn can also fire up when you:

• Bend forward

• Exercise

• Strain muscles

Why Acid Backs Up

Occasionally the acid keeps on coming until you have a mouthful of something bitter and acidy. You may have some pain in your gut, too, or in your chest. Along with that acid may come a belch, one that may bring even more of that stomach acid with it.

The purpose of stomach acid is to break down the foods we eat so our body can digest them. Our stomachs have a protective lining that shields it from those acids, but the esophagus does not have that protection. Normally that's not a problem because after we swallow food, it passes down the esophagus, through a sphincter, and into the stomach. The sphincter then closes.

Occasionally, though, the muscles of that sphincter are weakened and it doesn't close properly or it doesn't close all the way. Scarring from an ulcer or frequent episodes of acid reflux (when the acid comes back up), stomach pressure from overeating, obesity, and pregnancy can all cause this glitch in the lower esophageal sphincter (LES). And

WHEN TO CALL THE DOCTOR

- If you've tried home remedies or over-the-counter medications and they're not working. Your heartburn could be a symptom of another ailment, such as an ulcer, gallbladder disease, or hiatal hernia.

- If heartburn happens on a prolonged or regular basis, even if home treatments are working

- Call 9-1-1 or go to the nearest emergency room if you're have chest pain that spreads into your arm, jaw, or shoulder, especially if accompanied by any of these symptoms: sweating, nausea, dizziness, shortness of breath, fainting. This could be a heart attack.

FASCINATING FACT
Cold beverages may help cause heartburn. They cool down your stomach, which requires a certain amount of heat in order to function at its best.

when the LES gets a glitch and allows the gastric acid to splash out of the stomach, you get heartburn.

Generally, heartburn isn't serious. In fact, small amounts of reflux are normal and most people don't even notice it because the swallowing we do causes saliva to wash the acids right back down into the stomach where they belong. When the stomach starts shooting back amounts that are larger than normal, especially on a regular basis or over a prolonged period of time, that's when the real trouble begins, and simple heartburn can turn into esophageal inflammation or bleeding.

Who's prone to heartburn? Just about anybody. According to the National Digestive Diseases Clearinghouse, 25 million adults suffer from heartburn daily and about 60 million Americans get gastroesophageal reflux and heartburn at least once a month.

There are several prescription medicines available for the treatment of long-term or serious heartburn or acid reflux, and over-the-counter remedies are available at your pharmacy, too. But there are several remedies right in your own kitchen that can fight the fire of heartburn.

FROM THE CUPBOARD

ALMONDS. Chewing 6 or 8 blanched almonds during an episode of heartburn may relieve the symptoms. Chew them well, though, to avoid swallowing air and causing yourself more discomfort.

BAKING SODA. Take ½ teaspoon in ½ glass water. Check the antacid-use information on the box before using this remedy, however.

Warning! If you're on a salt-restricted diet, do not use baking soda. It's loaded with sodium. And do not use it if you're experiencing nausea, stomachache, gas, cramps, or stomach distention from overeating.

CREAM OF TARTAR. For an acid neutralizer, mix ½ teaspoon with ½ teaspoon baking soda in a glass of water. Take 1 teaspoon of the solution as needed.

BROWN RICE. Plain or with a little sweetening, rice can help relieve discomfort. Rice is a complex carbohydrate and is a bland food, which is less likely to increase acidity or relax the sphincter muscle.

SODA CRACKERS. This is an old folk cure that actually works. Soda crackers (preferably unsalted) are bland, they digest easily, and they absorb stomach acid. They also contain bicarbonate of soda and cream of tartar, which neutralize the acid. Tip: You know that package of soda crackers they always give you at the restaurant, that you leave on the table? From now on, take them with you. These come in handy when you're plagued by heartburn and are away from home.

FIRE-FIGHTING FOODS

Proteins may strengthen a weak sphincter that allows stomach acid to escape. Have some protein at every meal to keep that valve in good working order. These top the sphincter-friendly list:

- Lean meats
- Fish
- Poultry
- Low fat dairy products

VINEGAR. Mix 1 tablespoon apple cider vinegar, 1 tablespoon honey, and 1 cup warm water. Drink at the first sign of heartburn.

FROM THE DRAWER

PAPER AND PEN. Keep a food diary. This can tell you which foods or food combinations cause that heartburn.

FROM THE FAUCET

WATER. Drink water (or other beverages) in between meals, not with meals. If you drink fluids with meals, you increase the volume of stomach contents, which makes it easier for heartburn to occur.

FROM THE REFRIGERATOR

APPLES. They cool the burn of stomach acid. Eat them fresh, with the skin still on, or cook them for desserts.

APPLE HONEY. This is a simple remedy that will neutralize stomach acids. Peel, core, and slice several sweet apples. Simmer with a little water over low heat for three hours until the mixture is thick, brown, and sweet to the taste. Refrigerate in an airtight container and take a few spoonfuls whenever you have the need.

BUTTERMILK. This is an acid-reliever, but don't confuse it with regular milk, which can be an acid-maker, especially if you are bothered by lactose intolerance.

CABBAGE. Like apples, this is a natural fire extinguisher for stomach burn. For the best relief, put the cabbage through a juicer, then drink it.

FRUIT JUICES. Skip juices from citrus fruits, but try these stomach-cooling juices for heartburn relief: papaya, mango, guava, pear.

LIME JUICE. Mix 10 drops lime juice with ½ teaspoon sugar and ¼ teaspoon baking soda, in that order. When the baking soda is added it will fizz, and that's when you need to drink it down. The fizz will neutralize stomach acid.

PAPAYA. Eat it straight to reap the benefit of its natural, indigestion-fighting enzyme papain. Or drink 1 cup papaya juice combined with 1 teaspoon sugar and 2 pinches cardamom to relieve acid indigestion.

Warning! Pregnant women should not eat papayas; they're a source of natural estrogen that can cause a miscarriage.

POTATO. Mix ½ cup raw potato juice with ½ cup water, and drink after meals. To make raw potato juice, simply put a peeled raw potato through a juicer or blender.

PUMPKIN. Eat it baked as a squash to get rid of heartburn. Fresh is best. Spice it up with cinnamon, which is another heartburn cure. Or, make a compote of baked pumpkin and apples, spiced with cinnamon and honey, for a dessert that's both curative and tasty.

YOGURT. Make sure it has live cultures in it. Because of the helpful and digestive-friendly microorganisms in yogurt, it may soothe the acid-forming imbalances that can lead to heartburn.

FROM THE SPICE RACK

CARDAMOM. This old-time digestive aid may help relieve the burn of acid indigestion. Add it to baked goodies such as sweet rolls or fruit cake, or sprinkle, with a pinch of cinnamon, on toast. It works well in cooked cereals, too.

CINNAMON. This spice is a traditional remedy for acid relief. Brew a cup of cinnamon tea from a cinnamon stick.

Recipe
Box

SAGE TEA

2½ cups boiling water
¼ cup fresh sage leaves
1 teaspoon sugar or honey
juice of ½ lemon

Combine ingredients and steep for 20 minutes. Strain and drink warm.
The best relief comes from small, frequent doses.

Or try a commercial brand, but check the label. Cinnamon tea often has black tea in it, which is a cause of heartburn, so make sure your commercial brand doesn't contain black tea. For another acid-busting treat, make cinnamon toast.

GINGER. A tea from this root can soothe that burning belly. Add 1½ teaspoons gingerroot to 1 cup water; simmer for ten minutes. Drink as needed.

SAGE. For a tea that can relieve stomach weakness that allows acid to be released back into the esophagus, see the Recipe Box above.

MORE DO'S & DON'TS

- If you're carrying extra pounds, lose them. All that baggage pushing in on the abdomen increases pressure on the stomach, which causes heartburn.

- Eat smaller meals. The more food in your belly, the more likely that bulk will push stomach acid right back up.

- Eat slowly, chew thoroughly. Sometimes heartburn will flare because the food is simply too large to get through the digestive tract and it, along with the acids, is forced back up.

- Don't eat right before bedtime. Give your stomach a two- or three-hour break before you sleep. And if you're plagued by the burn at night, sleep with your head elevated on pillows.

- Let the gravity be with you. Stay upright so the gastric contents are forced to stay down. In other words, don't head for the couch after you eat. If you must snooze, try the recliner, but don't recline too steeply.

- Loosen your belt. Tight clothing and belts can create enough pressure to cause heartburn.

GUMMY FACTS

Gum-chewers are notorious air-swallowers. And air-swallowers are prone to indigestion. So if you're a gum-chewer who gets frequent indigestion, skip the gum for a while to see if there's a connection.

If you already are suffering with a bout of heartburn, however, chewing sugarless gum can bring relief. It increases the flow of saliva, which washes down the acid. Skip the mint flavors and don't chew too vigorously because that can lead to air-swallowing.

- Stay in shape. Heartburn hates people who are fit. However, skip strenuous exercise for a couple hours after a meal. Instead, go for a nice leisurely walk. This helps keep the stomach acid in its place.

- Stay calm. Stress increases acid production.

Heart Disease
Tending Your Ticker

The heart is an amazing struc-
ture, tough yet fragile. A muscle, its network of arteries
and veins transport blood
through your body, nourishing organs and tissues. When
the heart is working as it
should, you barely notice it. But
when your heart starts acting
strangely, you have cause to worry.

Thankfully, you live in a day when heart disease can be
treated very successfully, and in some cases, the condition
can even be reversed.

Heart Trouble

Heart disease is any condition that keeps your heart
from functioning at its best or causes a deterioration of
the heart's arteries and vessels. Coronary heart disease
(CHD), also known as coronary artery disease, is the most
common form of heart disease, affecting 12.6 million
people in America. If you are diagnosed with CHD, it
means you have atherosclerosis, or hardening of the arteries on the heart's surface. Arteries become hard when
plaque accumulates on artery walls. This plaque develops
gradually as an overabundance of low-density lipoprotein

(LDL) cholesterol (the bad stuff) makes itself at home in your arteries. The plaque builds and narrows the artery walls, making it more and more difficult for blood to pass through the heart and increasing the opportunity for a blood clot to form. If the heart doesn't get enough blood, it can cause chest pain (angina) or a heart attack.

Not treating coronary heart disease can also lead to congestive heart failure (CHF). CHF happens when your heart isn't strong enough to pump blood throughout the body— it fails to meet the body's need for oxygen. This often causes congestion in the lungs and a variety of other problems for your heart and the rest of your body.

> ## WHEN TO CALL THE DOCTOR
> - If you have any symptoms in "How to Know If You Have Heart Disease," pages 120–121 However, if you have any of the following symptoms, go to the nearest emergency room or call 9-1-1 immediately.
> - Painful pressure or squeezing in the chest that lasts for a few minutes or goes away and returns
> - Pain that radiates to the shoulders, neck, or arms
> - Lightheadedness, fainting, sweating, nausea, or shortness of breath along with chest pain

Honing In on Heart Disease

There are many risk factors for heart disease, some you can do something about and some you can't. A family history of heart disease puts you at much greater risk for developing it yourself. While you can't do anything about your genes, there are a number of risk factors that you can control. These are the ones you can do something about:

- High levels of low-density lipoprotein (LDL) cholesterol (the bad stuff), and low levels of high-density lipoprotein (the good stuff). (See High Cholesterol, page 136.)

- High levels of triglycerides. Triglyceride levels increase when you eat too many fatty foods or when you eat too much—excess calories are made into triglycerides and stored as fat in cells. Having an abundance of triglycerides has been linked to coronary heart disease.

- High blood pressure (see High Blood Pressure, page 129)

- Smoking

- Lack of regular exercise

- A high fat diet

- Being overweight or obese

- Diabetes (see Diabetes, page 70)

- Ongoing stress or depression

How to Know If You Have Heart Disease

About 25 to 30 percent of people who have heart disease don't even know it until something serious happens. That's why you should see your doctor for a checkup and have your cholesterol and triglyceride levels and your blood pressure checked and monitored. If you have any of the following symptoms, schedule a checkup right away:

- Chest pain (angina). If you feel like you have an elephant sitting on your chest after climbing the stairs, your body could be giving you a warning signal.

- Shortness of breath. This is especially noticeable after a game of one-on-one with your daughter or an intense meeting with your boss.

- Nausea or stomach upset. This could be more than the guacamole you ate at dinner, especially if you have recurrent bouts of tummy trouble.

- Sweating. Even when you haven't been exercising.

- Feeling weak or tired.

FROM THE CUPBOARD

BRAN. Bran cereal is a high-fiber food that will help keep your cholesterol levels in check. Other high-fiber foods in your cupboard include barley, oats, whole grains such as brown rice and lentils, and beans, such as kidney beans and black beans.

OLIVE OIL. The American Heart Association and the American Dietetic Association recommend getting most of your fat from monounsaturated sources. Olive oil is a prime candidate. Try using it instead of other vegetable oils when sautéing your veggies.

PEANUT BUTTER. Eat 2 tablespoons of this comforting food and you can get ⅓ of your daily intake of vitamin E. Because vitamin E is a fat-soluble vitamin (other antioxidant vitamins are water soluble), it is found more abundantly in fattier foods such as vegetable oils and nuts. If you're watching your weight, don't go overboard on the peanut butter.

PECANS. These tasty nuts are full of magnesium, another heart-friendly nutrient. One ounce of pecans drizzled over a spinach salad can give you ⅓ of your recommended daily allowance of this vital mineral.

WHOLE-WHEAT BREAD. Slather some peanut butter on a slice of whole-wheat bread and you've got a snack that's good to your heart. One slice of whole-wheat bread has

11 mcg of selenium, an antioxidant mineral that works with vitamin E to protect your heart.

WINE. Research is finding that drinking a glass of alcohol a day may help in the battle against heart disease. Health experts are quick to note that alcohol in moderate amounts is helpful. They define moderate as one glass a day for women and two glasses of alcohol a day for men. What's in one drink? Twelve ounces of beer, five ounces of wine, or 1.5 ounces of whiskey.

FROM THE REFRIGERATOR

BROCCOLI. Calcium is another heart-healthy nutrient, and milk isn't the only calcium-rich food. In fact, there are lots of nondairy foods that are rich in calcium, such as kale, salmon, figs, pinto beans, and okra. One cup of broccoli can supply you with 90 mg of calcium.

CHICKEN. Three ounces of chicken will give you ⅓ of your daily requirement for vitamin B_6, a necessary nutrient for maintaining heart health.

SALMON. Adding fatty fish to your diet is a good idea if you're at risk for heart disease. Three ounces of salmon meets your daily requirement for vitamin B_{12}, a vitamin that helps keep your heart healthy, and it's a good source of omega-3 fatty acids, which have been proven to lower triglycerides and reduce blood clots that could potentially block arteries in the heart.

SPINACH. Make yourself a salad using spinach instead of the usual iceberg lettuce and get a good start on meeting your folic acid needs (½ cup has 130 mcg of folic acid). Along with the other B vitamins, B_6 and B_{12}, folic acid can help prevent heart disease.

STRAWBERRIES. Oranges aren't the only fruit loaded with vitamin C. You can fill up on 45 mg of the heart healthy vitamin with ½ cup of summer's sweet berry. Vitamin C is an antioxidant vital to maintaining a happy heart. Strawberries are also a good source of fiber and potassium, both important to heart health.

SWEET POTATOES. With double your daily requirements for vitamin A, a heart-protecting nutrient, sweet potatoes are a smart choice for fending off heart disease.

FROM THE SPICE RACK

GARLIC. Chock full of antioxidants, garlic seems to be able to lessen plaque buildup, reduce the incidence of chest pain, and keep the heart generally healthy. It is also a mild anticoagulant, helping to thin the blood. However, it may take some time to reap the benefits: One study found that it took a couple of years of eating garlic daily to get its heart-healthy benefits.

FROM THE SUPPLEMENT SHELF

COENZYME Q-10. This nutrient, found in fatty fish, has a bit of an identity crisis. It's not classified as a vitamin or a mineral. But studies have found that it is a necessary nutrient for heart health. It seems that coenzyme Q-10 re-energizes heart cells, especially in people who have already been diagnosed with heart failure. It blocks the process that creates plaque buildup in the arteries and helps lower blood pressure. Coenzyme Q-10 has been used to treat congestive heart failure in Japan for decades. Talk to your doctor before trying the supplement. If you get the go-ahead, buy supplements from Japanese manufacturers.

More Do's and Don'ts

- Don't be a smokestack. People who smoke are twice as likely to have a heart attack.

- Get moving. Your heart is a muscle, and if you don't exercise it, it will get weaker and be less able to rebound from heart troubles.

- Watch your weight. The American Heart Association (AHA) says that if you're overweight, losing as little as 10 to 20 pounds can work wonders on your heart.

- Eat healthy. The AHA suggests getting less than 30 percent of your calories from fat, and less than 10 percent of that fat should be the saturated kind. You should get no more than 300 mg of cholesterol a day.

Hemorrhoids
DEALING WITH DISCOMFORT

Hemorrhoids are a sore subject, and not one that is brought up at the dinner table. Yet privately, millions of people suffer from these painful protrusions. Also known as piles, hemorrhoids are swollen, stretched out veins that line the anal canal and lower rectum. Internal hemorrhoids may either bulge into the anal canal or protrude out through the anus (these are called prolapsed). External hemorrhoids occur under the surface of the skin near the anal opening. Both types hurt, burn, itch, irritate, and bleed.

About one-half to three-fourths of Americans will develop hemorrhoids in their lifetime. Most cases are caused by constipation or physical strain while making a bowel movement. Other causes include heredity, age, a low-fiber diet resulting in constipation, obesity, the improper use of laxatives, pregnancy, anal intercourse, prolonged sitting, and prolonged standing.

Fortunately, most hemorrhoids respond well to home treatments and changes in the diet, so you can keep this sore point under wraps.

WHEN TO CALL THE DOCTOR

- If you have rectal bleeding. Although rectal bleeding is associated with hemorrhoids, it can also be a warning sign of colon and rectal cancer.
- If you are pregnant and develop hemorrhoids
- If you are in pain

FROM THE CUPBOARD

POTATO. A poultice made from grated potato works as an astringent and soothes pain. Take 2 washed potatoes, cut them into small chunks, and put them into a blender. Process until the potatoes are in liquid form. Add a few teaspoons water if they look dry. Spread the mashed taters into a thin gauze bandage or clean handkerchief, fold in half, and apply to the hemorrhoids for five to ten minutes.

Warning! Some folk remedies will have you placing raw potato pieces in places that don't see the light of day. Using potatoes or any other food as a suppository to help hemorrhoids should first be discussed with your physician.

PRUNES. If you haven't eaten a prune since your mother tried to force one down your throat at age five, then it's time to try again. As mama knew, prunes have a laxative effect and help soften stools. Try to eat 1 to 3 a day, and look at it as pleasure, not punishment.

VINEGAR. Applying a dab of apple cider or plain vinegar to hemorrhoids stops itching and burning. The vinegar has astringent properties that help shrink swollen blood vessels. After dry wiping, dip a cotton ball in vinegar and apply.

FROM THE FREEZER

ICE. Now here's a remedy guaranteed to wake you up and soothe hemorrhoid pain. Sit on a cold compress. That's right, literally freeze your rear end. Break ice into small cubes (easier for the ice to shape itself around certain regions), and place it in a plastic, resealable bag. Cover with a thick paper towel and sit on it! The cooling works twofold: First, it numbs the region, and second, it reduces blood flow to those distended veins.

FROM THE REFRIGERATOR

ORANGES. Vitamin C plays a role in strengthening and toning blood vessels, so eat lots of vitamin C-rich fruits and vegetables.

THE HEALING BENEFITS OF WITCH HAZEL

Witch hazel has long been used as a soothing, cooling astringent for hemorrhoid pain, itching, and bleeding. It has anti-inflammatory properties and, when applied to hemorrhoids, tightens up the tissues and stanches bleeding. A dab of witch hazel applied to the outer rectum with a cotton ball (after dry wiping) is one of the best and easiest remedies available for external hemorrhoids. Give your hemorrhoids a cool treat by keeping a bottle of witch hazel refrigerated. You can also make a compress soaked in witch hazel and leave it on your bottom while resting.

FROM THE SINK

WATER. Think of water as the plumber of the digestive tract, without the $85-an-hour fee. Water keeps the digestive process moving along without block-ups—one of the main causes of hemorrhoids. Reaping the benefits requires a minimum of 8 large glasses of water each day. Drinking other fluids, such as juice, and eating plenty of water-loaded fruits and vegetables can help the flow of things.

FROM THE WINDOWSILL

ALOE VERA. Versatile aloe vera comes to the rescue once again, this time as a hemorrhoid healer. The very same anti-inflammatory constituents that reduce blistering and inflammation in burns also help reduce the irritation of hemorrhoids. Break off a piece of the aloe vera leaf and apply only the clear gel to the hemorrhoids.

MORE DO'S AND DON'TS

- Be kind to your posterior by taking a nice soak in the tub. A bath does much to soothe inflamed tissues and ease pain. If you have hemorrhoids, it's recommended that you take a sitz bath three to four times a day for 30 minutes. Since this time commitment is often an impossibility for active people and working adults, try a mini-soak. Apply a washcloth moistened with warm water to the hemorrhoids for a few minutes a few times a day.

- Don't burst a blood vessel. Try to make a bowel movement without straining. If you don't have the urge to go, get off the pot. Along those same lines, don't be a bathroom reader and sit on the throne for hours in anticipation.

- Exercise. Regular aerobic exercise helps the digestive system work more efficiently.

- Easy does it. After a bowel movement, don't vigorously clean yourself with dry toilet paper. Buy premoistened wipes designed for anal care or, after gently wiping with toilet paper, apply witch hazel to clean yourself.

High Blood Pressure

REVERSING THE TREND

Sometimes what you don't know can hurt you. Such is the case with high blood pressure, or hypertension. Although one in four adults has high blood pressure, according to the American Heart Association (AHA), almost a third of them don't know they have it.

That's because high blood pressure often has no symptoms. It's not as if you feel the pressure of your blood coursing through your circulatory system. When the heart beats, it pumps blood to the arteries, creating pressure within them. That pressure can be normal or it can be excessive. High blood pressure is defined as a persistently elevated pressure of blood within the arteries.

Over time, the excessive force exerted against the arteries damages and scars them. It can also damage organs, such as the heart, kidneys, and brain. High blood pressure can lead to strokes, blindness, kidney failure, and heart failure.

In 90 to 95 percent of all cases, the cause of high blood pressure isn't known. In such cases, when there is no underlying cause, the disease is known as primary, or

WHEN TO CALL THE DOCTOR

- If you have a sudden weight change
- If you have palpitations
- If you have swelling in your extremities
- If you become dizzy or unsteady
- If you have sudden, severe headaches
- If you develop chest pain or a cough that does not go away

essential, hypertension. Sometimes the high blood pressure is caused by another disease, such as an endocrine disorder. In such cases the disease is called secondary hypertension.

Who's at Risk?

While no one knows the exact cause of hypertension, there are specific factors that put you at risk of developing it. These include:

Age. The older you are, the greater the likelihood of developing hypertension.

Weight. The heavier you are, the greater your risk of hypertension.

Race. African Americans are more prone to high blood pressure than Caucasians.

Heredity. If high blood pressure runs in your family, you have an increased chance of developing it.

Alcohol use. Heavy drinking increases blood pressure.

Sodium consumption. Too much salt in your diet will do you in if you're sodium sensitive.

A sedentary lifestyle. Couch potatoes are at an increased risk for hypertension.

Pregnancy. Some expectant mothers experience elevated blood pressure.

AMERICAN HEART ASSOCIATION RECOMMENDED BLOOD PRESSURE LEVELS			
BLOOD PRESSURE CATEGORY	SYSTOLIC (MM HG)	DIASTOLIC (MM HG)	FOLLOW-UP RECOMMENDED
Optimal	less than 120*	and less than 80*	Recheck in 2 years
Normal	less than 130	and less than 85	Recheck in 2 years
High normal	130–139	or 85–89	Recheck in 1 year
High			
Stage 1 (mild)	140–159	or 90–99	Confirm within 2 months
Stage 2 (moderate)	160–179	or 100–109	Evaluate within 1 month
Stage 3 (severe)	180 or higher	or 110 or higher	Evaluate immediately

Your doctor should evaluate unusually low readings.

Oral contraceptives. Some women who take birth control pills develop hypertension, especially if other risk factors are also present.

What to Look For

Hypertension is known as the silent killer because it has no or few obvious symptoms. The symptoms that it does present are shared by other diseases and conditions. But if you have any of these symptoms, be sure to have your blood pressure checked to rule out high blood pressure:

• Frequent or severe headaches

• Unexplained fatigue

• Dizziness

- Flushing of the face
- Ringing in the ears
- Thumping in the chest
- Frequent nosebleeds

Diagnosis

Finding out whether you have high blood pressure is simple. You just need to have your blood pressure checked by a doctor, nurse, or other health professional. Oftentimes you can even find blood pressure check booths at your local mall or at the pharmacy. The blood pressure test is simple, quick, and painless, but the results can save your life.

A blood pressure reading is given in two numbers, one over the other. The higher (systolic) number represents the pressure while the heart is beating, indicating how hard your heart has to beat to get that blood moving. The lower (diastolic) number represents the pressure when the heart is resting between beats.

Blood pressure of less than 140 (systolic) over 90 (diastolic) is considered a normal reading for adults, according to the AHA, while a reading equal to or greater than 140 over 90 is considered elevated (high). A systolic pressure of 130 to 139 or a diastolic pressure of 85 to 89 needs to be watched carefully.

The key to controlling high blood pressure is knowing you have it. Under the guidance of a physician, you can battle hypertension through diet, exercise, lifestyle changes, and medication, if necessary. The kitchen holds several blood pressure helpers.

FROM THE COUNTER

BANANAS. The banana has been proved to help reduce blood pressure. The average person needs three to four servings of potassium-rich fruits and vegetables each day. Some experts believe doubling this amount may benefit your blood pressure. If bananas aren't your favorite bunch of fruit, try dried apricots, raisins, currants, orange juice, spinach, boiled potatoes with skin, baked sweet potatoes, cantaloupe, and winter squash.

FROM THE CUPBOARD

BREADS. Be good to your blood with a bit more B, as in the B vitamin folate. Swimming around the blood is a substance called homocysteine, which at high levels is thought to reduce the stretching ability of the arteries. If the arteries are stiff as a board, the heart pumps extra hard to move the blood around. Folate helps reduce the levels of homocysteine, in turn helping arteries become pliable. You'll find folate in fortified breads and cereals, asparagus, brussels sprouts, and beans.

CANOLA, MUSTARD SEED, OR SAFFLOWER OILS. Switching to polyunsaturated oils can make a big difference in your blood pressure readings. Switching to them will also help reduce your blood cholesterol level.

FROM THE REFRIGERATOR

BROCCOLI. This vegetable is high in fiber, and a high-fiber diet is known to help reduce blood pressure. So indulge in this and other fruits and vegetables that are high in fiber.

CELERY. Because it contains high levels of 3-N-butylph-thalide, a phytochemical that helps lower blood pressure, celery is in a class by itself. This phytochemical is not

TASTY, NOT SALTY

Americans nearly preserve themselves with salt. The average American consumes between 3,000 and 6,000 mg of sodium each day. (The maximum intake suggested is 2,400 mg, which is about the amount in a level teaspoon of salt.)

A diet high in salt, or sodium chloride, is directly linked to high blood pressure in salt-sensitive individuals, so start on the road to lower blood pressure by waving bye-bye to the saltshaker. There are several salt-free substitutes you can purchase, or you can make your own salt-free substitute that will spice up your meals without compromising your health.

found in most other vegetables. Celery may also reduce stress hormones that constrict blood vessels, so it may be most effective in those whose high blood pressure is the result of mental stress.

MILK. The calcium in milk does more than build strong bones; it plays a modest role in preventing high blood pressure. Be sure to drink skim milk or eat low fat yogurt. Leafy green vegetables also provide calcium.

FROM THE SPICE RACK

CAYENNE PEPPER. This fiery spice is a popular home treatment for mild high blood pressure. Cayenne pepper allows smooth blood flow by preventing platelets from clumping together and accumulating in the blood. Add some cayenne pepper to salt-free seasonings, or add a dash to a salad or salt-free soup.

FROM THE SUPPLEMENT SHELF

VITAMIN C. An antioxidant, vitamin C helps prevent damage to artery walls, and it may help improve high blood pressure. Take a vitamin C supplement or eat foods rich in this nutrient.

MORE DO'S AND DON'TS

- Do aerobic exercise. Aerobic exercise that elevates your pulse and sustains the elevation for at least 20 minutes will help reduce your blood pressure if you do it several times a week. It will also help you lose weight, which will help lower your blood pressure. Check with your doctor before starting an exercise program if you've been sedentary.

- Avoid strength training exercise, such as weight lifting, unless you first consult with your doctor. This kind of exercise can be dangerous for people with hypertension.

- Lose the saltshaker. Although there is some debate about salt's role in high blood pressure, most experts agree that cutting back on salt intake can reduce blood pressure.

- Quit smoking. Smoking causes blood pressure to rise and it increases your risk of stroke.

- Skip processed foods. They are loaded with sodium (salt) and high in saturated (read: artery-clogging) fat. Read labels, as it's not always obvious which foods contain the most sodium and saturated fat.

High Cholesterol
LOWERING THE NUMBERS

Cholesterol is that
waxy, soft stuff that
floats around in your
bloodstream as well
as in all the cells
in your body. It
takes a bad rap
these days because

the word cholesterol strikes fear in the hearts of even the
healthiest of people.

Having cholesterol in your blood is normal and even
healthy because it's used in the formation of cell membranes, tissues, and essential hormones. So, in proper
amounts, cholesterol is good. In excessive amounts,
though, it can clog the arteries leading to your heart and
cause coronary disease, heart attack, or stroke.

Cholesterol comes from two sources: the foods you eat
and your very own liver. And the truth of the matter is,
your liver can produce all the cholesterol your body will
ever need. This means that what you get in your food isn't
necessary. Some people get rid of extra cholesterol easily
through normal bodily waste mechanisms, but others
hang on to it because their bodies just aren't as efficient in
removing it, which puts them at risk.

So, what makes people prone to having high blood cholesterol?

- Family history
- Eating too many foods high in saturated fats
- Diabetes
- Kidney and liver disorders
- Alcoholism
- Obesity
- Smoking
- Stress

Good and Bad Cholesterol?

There are two different kinds of cholesterol, and yes, one's good and one's bad. Cholesterol can't get around on its own, so it hitches a ride from lipoproteins to get to the body's cells. Problem is, there are two different rigs picking it up: One is called HDL, or high-density lipoprotein, and the other is called LDL, or low-density lipoprotein. HDL is the good ride; it travels away from your arteries. LDL is the bad

WHEN TO CALL THE DOCTOR

Call 9-1-1 for:

- Crushing chest pain, possibly accompanied by nausea, vomiting, shortness of breath, sweating, weakness
- Dull chest pain or a feeling of tightness or heavy pressure
- Pain that starts in the chest, possibly radiating to the arms and jaw
- Symptoms of stroke: loss of speech, balance problems, sudden weakness or paralysis on one side of the body, sudden vision problems, numbness in your extremities

Call the doctor for:

- Weakness or pain in the buttocks, legs, or feet during exertion
- Feet that never warm up
- Leg or foot sores that won't heal
- Discolored skin on legs and feet
- Sharp, sudden leg or foot pain during rest

ride; it heads straight to your arteries. Bottom line: HDL is what you want more of; you want less of LDL.

High cholesterol can be cured two ways: by medication and/or by diet. There are numerous effective drugs on the market that will make drastic reductions in cholesterol levels, but they all come with side effects and require frequent blood tests to monitor for possible problems. But there are kitchen cures, and they may work on their own or along with conventional medical treatment. Whatever your cure, it must come with advice from your doctor since your heart is at risk.

FROM THE COUNTER

GARLIC. Studies show that garlic may not only reduce LDL but raise HDL and decrease the amount of fat in your blood. Add some fresh garlic regularly to your cooking to keep your heart healthy.

FROM THE CUPBOARD

ALMONDS. Studies indicate that snacking on almonds regularly for as little as three weeks may decrease LDL by up to ten percent.

HONEY. Add 1 teaspoon honey to 1 cup hot water in the morning, and you may rid your system of excess fat and cholesterol, according to Ayurvedic medicine. Add 1 teaspoon lime juice or 10 drops cider vinegar to give that drink a more powerful cholesterol-fighting punch.

OATS. In any pure form, oats are a traditional cholesterol buster. Eating only ½ cup oatmeal a day, along with a low fat diet, may reduce cholesterol levels by nine percent.

RICE. The oil that comes from the bran of rice is known to lower cholesterol. And brown rice is particularly high in fiber, which is essential to include in a cholesterol-lowering diet. One cup provides 11 percent of the daily fiber requirement.

> ### FASCINATING FACT
> The egg yolk has 213 milligrams of cholesterol, but the white has 0. In recipes that call for an egg, cut out the cholesterol by using 2 egg whites in place of 1 whole egg.

SOYBEANS. These beauties may reduce LDL by as much as 20 percent when 25 to 50 grams of soy protein are eaten daily for as short a time as a month. Besides that obvious benefit, soy may fend off a rise in LDL in people with normal levels and also improve the ability of arteries to dilate. This means they expand better to allow the unimpeded passage of fats and other substances that otherwise might cause a blockage.

WALNUTS. A cholesterol-lowering diet that includes walnuts eaten at least four times a week may lower LDL by as much as 16 percent. And studies indicate that those who munch on these nuts regularly cut their risk of dying from a heart attack in half when compared to non-walnut munchers.

FROM THE DRAWER

CALCULATOR. Add up those cholesterol milligrams daily to see how you're doing.

NOTEBOOK. Chart your daily diet.

NUTRITION & FOOD GUIDE. Use it to gauge the cholesterol content of the foods you eat. Record the results.

FAT FACT

The more liquid the margarine (tub, liquid form), the less hydrogenated it is and the less trans fatty acid it contains. Trans fatty acids raise total blood cholesterol levels, so the less of them you eat, the better off you are.

FROM THE REFRIGERATOR

ALFALFA SPROUTS. These may improve or normalize cholesterol levels.

Warning! Sprouts are not clean or washed when you buy them in the store, and they may be a source of *E. coli* bacteria. Wash thoroughly before you consume or use a veggie-cleaning product available in most grocery stores.

APPLES. Apples are high in pectin, which can lower cholesterol levels.

ARTICHOKES. This veggie can actually lower cholesterol levels. Early studies pointed to their beneficial cholesterol-busting properties, but recent studies have shown that artichokes may be even more effective than they were first thought to be.

BEETS. Full of carotenoids and flavonoids, beets help lower—and may even prevent—the formation of LDL, the bad cholesterol.

CARROTS. Full of pectin, they're as good as apples in lowering cholesterol levels.

OLIVE OIL. It protects your heart by lowering LDL, raising HDL, and preventing your blood from forming clots.

PEARS. These are high in soluble fiber, which helps regulate cholesterol levels.

RHUBARB. Yep, this is a cholesterol-buster. Consume it after a meal that's heavy in fats. You can cook it in a double boiler, with a little honey or maple syrup for added sweetness, until done. Add cardamom or vanilla if you like.

YOGURT. Eating 1 cup plain yogurt with active cultures a day may reduce LDL by four percent or more and total cholesterol by at least three percent. Some scientists believe that eating yogurt regularly may even reduce the overall risk of heart disease by as much as ten percent.

> ### FASCINATING FACTS
> - 20 percent of all Americans have high blood cholesterol.
> - 33 percent have borderline high levels.

FROM THE SPICE RACK

TURMERIC. This may lower blood cholesterol. Added to eggplant, you may reap twice the cholesterol-fighting benefit. Mix ¾ teaspoon turmeric with 2 tablespoons cooked, mashed eggplant and 1½ tablespoons boiling water. Spread it on whole wheat bread and eat after a meal heavy in fats.

MORE DO'S & DON'TS

- Don't grease those pans. Use a nonstick olive oil spray or buy an inexpensive oil mister in a kitchenware store and make your own spray.

- Bulk up. Whole grains are high in fiber. Complex carbohydrates fill you up faster and leave you feeling satisfied. Try eating more fruits, veggies, pasta, and rice.

- Exercise. Regular exercise can boost HDL.

- Read food labels. They list the cholesterol content, so remember your cholesterol goal: less than 300 mg a day.

- Eat small meals. Instead of three big meals a day, go for five or six small meals. The body deals with cholesterol intake more efficiently when it comes in small amounts.

Insomnia/Sleep Disorders

RECLAIMING YOUR REST

The house is completely quiet. The kids are in bed. Your hubby is sawing logs. But you are staring at the ceiling listening to the fan hum. You've tried everything: counting sheep, counting dots on the ceiling, reading *War and Peace,* watching old sitcoms. But nothing is working. So you resign yourself to another dreary day of being a poster child for the walking dead.

Thirty to forty million Americans have some sort of trouble sleeping. There are more than 60 sleep disorders that plague men and women, from sleep apnea to restless legs syndrome. The number one sleep problem for men and women is insomnia. The National Sleep Foundation reports that 48 percent of Americans have insomnia occasionally, and 22 percent deal with sleeplessness almost every night. This wouldn't be such an unsettling statistic if lack of sleep was no big deal. But your body and mind need to shut down for a while at the end of the day.

Insufferable Insomnia

Insomnia can be classified in one of three ways—trouble falling asleep (called sleep-onset insomnia), trouble staying asleep (this is called sleep-maintenance insomnia), or waking up feeling groggy and sleepy after what should have been a full night's sleep. Most episodes of insomnia last anywhere from a couple of nights to a few weeks. There are myriad causes, including stress, anxiety, depression, disease, pain, medications, or simply not creating a relaxing sleep routine.

WHEN TO CALL THE DOCTOR

- If your sleep problems last for three weeks
- If your sleep problems impact your ability to function during the day
- If you continually have to get up several times a night to urinate
- If you can't stay in bed because you need to keep moving your legs

There's no magic number when it comes to how many hours you should sleep. Some people get by just fine on a few hours, and some people need more than eight. But it won't be a mystery to you if you're not getting enough sleep. Waking up exhausted and being sleepy most of the day are signs that you're not well-rested.

Suffering Through Sleepless Nights

Women are 1.3 times more likely to experience insomnia than men. And people older than 65 are 1.5 times more likely to have trouble sleeping than someone younger. Marital problems make you more likely to have insomnia, as do hormonal changes such as those that occur during menopause, menstruation, and pregnancy.

Insomnia's Ill Effects

Insomnia can have a significant impact on your health and well-being. If you don't get enough sleep, you're setting yourself up for some serious problems. People with insomnia are

- Four times more likely to be diagnosed with depression.

- More likely to have a serious illness, including heart disease.

- More likely to have an accident on the job, at home, or on the road.

- More likely to miss work and accomplish less on the job than well-rested coworkers.

FROM THE CUPBOARD

COOKIES. Yes, that comforting nighttime snack of milk and cookies may be just what the doctor ordered to get you back in bed. Sugary foods eaten about 30 minutes before bedtime can actually act as a sedative, and you can wake up without the morning fuzziness that accompanies synthetic sleeping pills. Be careful to eat only a few cookies, though; eating too much sugar at bedtime can keep the sandman at bay.

EPSOM SALTS. Naturopathic practitioners recommend this remedy for sleepless nights. Add 1 to 2 cups Epsom salts to a hot bath and soak for about 15 to 20 minutes before hitting the hay.

HONEY. Folk remedies often advise people with sleeping difficulty to eat a little honey. It has the same sedative effect as sugar and may get you to bed more quickly. Try adding 1 tablespoon honey to some decaffeinated herbal

WHEN YOUR LEGS WANT TO DO SOME WALKING...BUT YOU WANT TO SLEEP

Restless legs syndrome is a frustrating condition. The name of the problem explains it all. When you finally get into bed, your legs decide it's time to get up and move. The symptoms of restless legs syndrome have been described as tingling, crawling, or prickling sensations that peak during times of inactivity, such as when you're trying to go to sleep. Walking, massaging your legs, or taking a hot shower can help relieve the problem for a bit, but it'll come back, leaving you with a sleep-deprived night. Restless legs syndrome has been connected with a deficiency in iron and folic acid. The problem worsens with age and is more frequently diagnosed in people over 65. It can be treated with prescription medicines.

tea—or even to your warm milk—for a relaxing pre-sleep drink.

TOAST. High-carbohydrate, low-protein bedtime snacks can make sleeping easier. Carbohydrate-rich foods tend to be easy on the tummy and can ease the brain into blissful slumber.

FROM THE REFRIGERATOR

MILK. Drinking a glass of milk, especially a glass of warm milk, before bedtime is an age-old treatment for sleeping troubles. There is some debate, however, about what it is in milk—if anything—that helps cause slumber. Some scientists believe it's the presence of tryptophan, a chemical that helps the brain ease into sleep mode, that does the trick. Others believe it may be another ingredient, a soothing group of opiatelike chemicals called casomorphins. Whatever the reason, milk seems to help some people hit the sack more easily. And warm milk seems to be more effective at relaxing body and mind. Other foods high on the tryptophan scale are cottage cheese, cashews, chicken, turkey, soybeans, and tuna.

FROM THE SPICE RACK

DILL SEED. Though scientists haven't proved its worth, this herb is often used as a folk cure for insomnia in China. Its essential oil has the most sedative-producing properties.

FROM THE SUPPLEMENT SHELF

5-HTP. Some experts believe a tryptophan deficiency can cause problems with sleep. Made from tryptophan, 5-HTP helps the body make serotonin. Low levels of serotonin are a known factor in sleepless nights. Taking a 5-HTP supplement may be a benefit if your body has low levels of tryptophan. How do you know if you're low? Low levels of tryptophan are most common in people who are depressed. If your insomnia is associated with depression, it might be a good question to ask your doctor. In one study, 100 mg of the supplement was enough to make sleep longer and better.

MELATONIN. Melatonin is the timekeeper of the body. It's a hormone that regulates your biological clock. As you get older you make less melatonin, which experts believe is probably why older folks have more trouble sleeping. Research is showing that taking a melatonin supplement can help you sleep. Ask your doctor about taking 1 to 3 mg of melatonin 1½ to 2 hours before bedtime.

MORE DO'S AND DON'TS

- Nix the nap. People who have trouble falling asleep or staying asleep shouldn't try to sleep during the day. It usually adds to the problem. If you are drooling over your keyboard and simply must have some rest, nap for no longer than 30 minutes early in the afternoon.

- Cut out the caffeine. Caffeine, by its nature, stimulates your brain. When you're trying to snooze, caffeine can cause problems. Having a couple of cups of coffee or a soda early in the day is fine, but switch to decaf after lunch.

- Avoid alcohol. Yes, alcohol is a sedative, but the effects soon wear off and you'll end up tossing and turning.

- Get physical. Exercise does help you sleep better, but watch when you do it. Exercise too close to bedtime and you may be too keyed up to rest. Try that early afternoon salsa class.

- Take it easy on yourself. Don't try so hard to get to sleep. If the sandman doesn't come 30 minutes after hitting the sack, get up and go to another room. Read a book or watch TV, do something relaxing, and try again when you're feeling sleepy.

- Create bedtime bliss. Make your bedroom as dark, quiet, and peaceful as you can, and reserve the bed for sleep and sex only.

- Maintain a relaxing routine. Try to do the same things before turning in. Take a hot bath or read a book, whatever relaxes you. This will help your brain prepare for a peaceful night's sleep.

Low Immunity
MARSHALING YOUR DEFENSES

In medical terms, having immunity means that you have resistance to infection or a specified disease. So if you have low immunity, it means your immune system isn't up to par and that you have a greater chance of getting the germ-du-jour. There are many factors that affect your body's response to a foreign invader, including how you're feeling at the moment you're introduced to a suspect germ. But if you consistently end up with the latest flu bug or stomach virus, your immune system may be running on empty.

The Battle for Your Body

Imagine your immune system as the front line in your body's war against foreign invaders. The vast network of glands, tissues, and cells are all soldiers working together to get rid of bacteria, viruses, parasites, and anything that invades their turf. The major troops in this war are the lymphatic system, made of the lymph nodes, thymus, spleen, and tonsils; white blood cells; and other specialized cells such as macrophages and mast cells. Each of these troops has a specialized job in enhancing the body's ability to fight off infection.

Lymph nodes are responsible for filtering out waste products from tissues throughout the body. Under the lymph nodes' command are cells that overtake bacteria and other potentially harmful foreign bodies and crush them like ants. That's why your lymph nodes swell up like golf balls when you are actively fighting off an infection.

WHEN TO CALL THE DOCTOR
- If you have more than 4 to 5 colds a year
- If you have a chronic or ongoing infection
- If you have lymph glands that swell, even when you don't feel bad
- If you now have, or have ever had, cancer. Ask your doctor to check for signs of an impaired immune system.

The thymus is your immune system's stealth warfare command center. You may not have heard of the thymus, but without it you would be one sick puppy. The thymus is a gland that produces many of those disease-fighting white blood cells—the foot soldiers that come to your defense against many types of infections. And the thymus produces hormones that enhance your immune function overall. So if your thymus isn't working as it should, your body may have trouble fighting off infection.

The spleen is vital to your immune defense. It produces white blood cells, kills bacteria, and enhances the immune system overall. White blood cells are your body's main defense in the battle against infection. White blood cells with names such as neutrophils, eosinophils, basophils, T cells, B cells, and natural killer cells, are all part of the vast army of disease assaulters.

When the Enemy Strikes

When something enters your body that is viewed by the immune system as harmful, your body goes into a state of heightened alert. When your immune system is healthy and all systems are go, these foreign invaders, or antigens, are typically met by a barrage of antibodies, which are produced by white blood cells. These antibodies latch on to antigens and set into action all the events that lead to the invader's eventual demise.

If things in your immune system are not working properly, you become less able to fight off those foreign invaders. Eventually they set up shop in your body and you get sick. An impaired immune system can make you more susceptible to colds and other merely frustrating illnesses, but it can also make you more at risk for developing cancer.

Science is proving that getting enough of the right nutrients can help you build your immune system. Scientific studies are discovering that avoiding something as simple as a cold or something as life threatening as cancer may be partially dependent upon what you stock in your kitchen.

FROM THE CUPBOARD

ALMONDS. Eat a handful of almonds for your daily dose of vitamin E; it's an immune-strengthening antioxidant. Studies have found that vitamin E deficiency substantially weakens the immune system.

CRAB. A zinc deficiency can zap your immune system. Zinc acts as a catalyst in the immune system's killer response to foreign bodies, and it protects the body from damage from invading cells. It is also a necessary ingredient for white blood cell function. Nosh on 3 ounces canned crab (or fresh) and you've got one-third of your recommended daily allowance (RDA) of this immune-enhancing nutrient.

NAVY BEANS. Everybody needs a little folic acid (it's the most common nutrient deficiency in the United States). And not getting enough of this vital nutrient can actually shrink vital immune system fighters like your thymus and lymph nodes. To make sure you're getting your fill of folic acid, try popping open a can of navy beans with dinner. One cup gets you half of your recommended daily allowance (RDA) of folic acid.

FROM THE FRUIT BASKET

GUAVA. Go a little tropical with this tasty fruit and get more than twice your daily vitamin C needs. Vitamin C acts as an immune enhancer by helping white blood cells perform at their peak and quickening the response time of the immune system.

FROM THE REFRIGERATOR

CHICKEN. Selenium is a trace mineral that is vital to the development and movement of white blood cells in the body. A 3-ounce piece of chicken will give you almost half your daily needs.

PORK. Not getting enough vitamin B_6 can keep your immune system from functioning at its best. Eating 3 ounces of lean roast pork will provide you with one-third of most adults' daily requirements for this immune-helping vitamin.

WINE. Have a glass of red wine and you may help your body take out a few potentially harmful foreign bodies. Certain components in wine seem to be helpful in killing infectious bacteria, such as *Salmonella*. But be careful. Drinking too much alcohol can cause your immune system to become depressed, leaving you more open to infection. A glass a day should do the trick.

YOGURT. Yogurt seems to have a marked effect on the immune system. It strengthens white blood cells and helps the immune system produce antibodies. One study found that people who ate 6 ounces of yogurt a day avoided colds, hay fever, and diarrhea. Another study found that yogurt could be an ally in the body's war against cancer.

FROM THE SUPPLEMENT SHELF

ECHINACEA. Research has shown echinacea can boost the body's immune response. It is particularly effective at fighting viral infections, such as the cold and flu, helping your body heal faster. Take 1 or 2 capsules or tablets up to three times a day. You can also buy dried echinacea and brew it into a tea. Simmer 1 to 2 teaspoons in 1 cup boiling water for 10 to 15 minutes; drink up to 3 cups a day.

FROM THE VEGETABLE BIN

CARROTS. Carotenes, like the beta-carotene found in carrots and other red, yellow, orange, and dark-green leafy vegetables, are the protectors of the immune system, specifically the thymus gland. Carotenes bolster white blood cell production, and numerous studies have shown

CAN MULTIVITAMINS MAKE YOU STRONGER?

Getting enough of essential nutrients is a good start on the road to a healthy immune system. And generally, eating a well-balanced diet will get you on that road. But you may be thinking about taking a multivitamin to help fill in the gaps. Are they worth it? And what should you look for?

Most nutrition experts would tell you to get the majority of your nutrients from food—mostly because there are other good-for-you components in food that a specific vitamin may not offer. Taking a multivitamin is a good backup plan. If you decide to take a multivitamin, follow these tips:

- Look for a vitamin/mineral combination. You need vitamins *and* minerals to enhance your immune system, so be sure the product you choose has all you need.
- Don't use products that have more than 100 percent of the recommended daily allowance (RDA) or daily value (DV) of a nutrient. You're going to get most of your vitamins and minerals from your diet, so don't go overboard.
- Make sure your multivitamin meets your needs. If you need to boost your immune system, look for a multivitamin that has the vitamins and minerals discussed in the "cures" section.
- Check the expiration date. Multivitamins may not start to smell after they expire, but they can lose their potency.
- Only take what is recommended. One a day is exactly what you should take. Don't double up on pills.

that eating foods rich in beta-carotene helps the body fight off infection more easily.

GARLIC. Garlic is well-known for its antibacterial and antiviral properties. It's even been thought to help prevent cancer. Researchers think these benefits stem from garlic's amazing effect on the immune system. One study found that people who ate more garlic had more of the natural killer white blood cells than those who didn't eat garlic.

KALE. A cup of kale will give you your daily requirement of vitamin A. Vitamin A is an antioxidant that helps your body fight cancer cells and is essential in the formation of white blood cells. Vitamin A also increases the ability of antibodies to respond to invaders.

SHIITAKE MUSHROOMS. Throw a few shiitake mushrooms in your stir-fry and you may prevent your yearly cold. Scientists have discovered that components of shiitake mushrooms have antiviral and immune-boosting properties.

MORE DO'S AND DON'TS

- Skip the sugar. Sugar may keep your white blood cells from being their strongest. Keep the sweet stuff to a minimum if your immune system isn't up to par.

- Forgo fat. Polyunsaturated fats in vegetable oils such as corn, safflower, and sunflower oil seem to be a deterrent to an efficiently running immune system.

- Lose a few pounds. Being overweight has a major effect on your immune system. One study found that the white blood cells in overweight people weren't as able to fight off infection as those of their healthy-weight peers.

- Try to relax. If stress causes you to lose your cool, you could be impairing your immune system. Chronic stress can even shrink your thymus gland, creating major problems in your body's ability to fight off infection. This is probably why you always seem to get a nasty cold during your busiest times at work.

- Add some activity. Exercise is a proven immune system booster. Don't overdo it, though. Too much can wear you down and create immune system problems.

Memory Problems
Sharpening Your Skills

Some events, and some names and faces, definitely should be forgotten. Embarrassing moments, things you wish you hadn't said or done, are memories you can relegate to the memory trash bin. Purposely forgetting is one thing, and we all try to do it on occasion. But on those occasions when memory simply fails you—when you truly don't remember a name, a job assignment slips your mind, you forget a doctor's appointment—your forgetfulness can have unpleasant consequences.

Forgetting is normal. We all experience it from time to time. And when it's an occasional problem, that's OK. But when forgetfulness becomes a chronic problem, that indicates that one of two things is happening:

1. You're not locking in the information you just received. New information will be lost in seven seconds if you don't lock it in right away.

2. You have a physical or mental condition that's preventing you from remembering. For example: Alzheimer's disease, senile dementia, hypoglycemia, severe anemia, depression, anxiety, alcohol or drug abuse, head injury, or

WHEN TO CALL THE DOCTOR

- If memory problems develop suddenly
- If memory problems frequently cause difficulty in everyday situations

severe viral or bacterial illness. Some prescribed medications make remembering a little difficult, too.

Memory is divided into two parts: short-term and long-term. The short-term memory bank holds the memory for only a few seconds, then transfers it to the long-term memory bank. If the transfer doesn't take place, the memory is completely lost.

If you're affected by the Seven-Second Syndrome, which is failing to lock in information once it's presented to you, there are memory-strengthening techniques that can improve that forgetfulness.

Mnemonics. This is the skill of consciously gathering new memory (information) and connecting it to prior memory (knowledge) for easy recall. For example, if you meet someone named Webster, it might trigger you to think of Webster's dictionary. You've now connected something new, the person's name, with something you already know. The connection itself is the mnemonic.

Acronyms. This is a word formed from a group of letters, each representing the first letter of a word that makes up a phrase. We're such an acronymic society that acronyms are assigned to just about everything, so why not join the crowd and assign your own acronyms to things you want to remember. An easy acronym that comes to mind is ASAP: as soon as possible. Maybe in your cooking, ASAP can mean add salt and pepper.

Rhymes. Rhyme and rhythm have always been terrific memory aids.

Lists, mental images, visual prompts. These all can help you forget your forgetfulness.

Sometimes memory problems stem from nutritional deficiencies, stress, and other problems that can be controlled once you know how. Here are some kitchen memory boosters that might just help you remember.

FROM THE CUPBOARD

PISTACHIO NUTS. If your memory loss is the result of a thiamine deficiency, pistachio nuts can help. One of the richest sources of thiamine, ½ cup pistachio nuts supplies 0.54 mg of thiamine. The RDA for thiamine is 1.5 mg for men and 1.1 mg for women age 50 and younger. Women older than 50 need slightly less.

WHEAT GERM. Wheat germ is a good source of vitamin E, which may help with age-related memory loss.

FROM THE DRAWER

PAPER. Create a food plan and keep a diary. Some foods enhance mental powers, but some make mental powers sluggish. Find out which food choices and combinations are best for you by charting your choices and their effects.

UTENSILS. You know what's supposed to be there, right? A whisk, a wooden spoon, a rolling pin, measuring cups. Chances are, your utensil drawer hasn't changed for years, so this is a great place to conduct a memory exercise. Take a good look, tidy the drawer to remind you what's there, then ask a friend or loved one to remove an item or two. Tomorrow, take a good look, tidy the drawer again, and see what's missing. This exercise will not only keep your memory on its toes, it will also keep that drawer in perfect order.

FROM THE KITCHEN TABLE

THE MORNING PAPER. Sit, relax, and turn to the crossword puzzle. This is a great way to exercise your brain and strengthen your memory.

RECIPE BOX. Memory is jogged by familiarity. Sit down at the table, relax, and think about a few favorite and familiar recipes. Try to recreate them from memory, writing down their ingredients and directions. Do the same tomorrow and the followin days, with the same recipes, and compare your results.

FROM THE REFRIGERATOR

ARTICHOKES. These are thought to increase your mental acuity. Prepare and eat them as you normally would or follow this recipe for an elixir of artichoke: Pull the artichoke apart, leaf by leaf, then put the pieces into a jar and add enough water to just barely cover. Cover the jar with a lid or saucer, and place in a pan with water. Boil for two hours, adding more water to the pan (not the jar) as necessary. Then strain the contents of the jar and give the artichoke leaves a good squeeze to get out all the juices. Take 3 to 4 tablespoons four times a day.

BLUEBERRIES. These luscious little fruits are the richest source of antioxidants, and recent studies have shown that blueberries may help improve short-term memory.

CARROTS. They contain carotene, which is a memory booster. Eat them raw, cooked, or in casseroles, or make a juice with carrots and apricots. The apricots are used to add a little compatible juice to the dry carrots.

EGGS. These have lecithin, which keeps the memory nerve cells healthy. Lecithin is also found in sunflower and soybean oils and can be purchased in capsule form, too. Studies indicate that taking up to 70 grams a day may improve memory.

> *FASCINATING FACT*
> The human brain uses more energy than any other organ in the human body. It makes up about 2 percent of total body weight but uses up to 20 percent of the body's total oxygen.

OKRA. If not a memorable food, this is at least a memory-enhancing one. So are sweet potatoes, tapioca, and spinach. Fresh fruits, especially oranges, and vegetables, almonds, and milk also stimulate your memory.

FROM THE SPICE RACK

ANISEED. Some herbalists suggest using aniseed to improve memory. Add 7 teaspoons aniseed to 1 quart boiling water, and let it simmer until it reduces by about half. Strain, and while still warm, add 4 teaspoons honey and 4 teaspoons glycerine, which can be purchased at the drugstore. Take 2 tablespoons three times a day.

HERBAL TEAS. Any of these will help a weak memory: sage, rosemary, marjoram, basil. Use ¼ teaspoon in a cup of boiling water. Steep for five minutes, strain, and drink. These herbs, in an essential oil, can be added to olive oil and massaged over the neck and forehead. Add these oils to bathwater, too: 5 drops to a tubful.

FROM THE SUPPLEMENT SHELF

VITAMIN B6. A deficiency in this vitamin, also called pyridoxine, can cause memory loss. Supplementation may improve memory in older adults.

VITAMIN E. Recent studies have reported improved short-term memory in older adults who took supplemental vitamin E.

MORE DO'S & DON'TS

• Write it down. Post notes. Keep lists. Mark it on the calendar.

• Exercise. This stimulates circulation, which is good for the brain.

• Meditate. The more you worry about memory loss, the more apt you are to suffer from it. Relax and think about other, more pleasant things.

Nausea/Vomiting

HALTING THE HEAVES

It happens to everybody, sometime. No one gets a free pass. But that doesn't make the misery of nausea and vomiting any easier on your system. Nausea is a warning signal; it means stop eating, let your stomach rest. Vomiting is a warning signal, too; it means something doesn't belong in your stomach and it's time to get rid of it. In other words, nausea and vomiting are two ways that your tummy protects itself.

Who Dunnit?

Usually nausea and vomiting are self-limiting: Once the cause is removed, the symptoms go away. So what causes these unsettling symptoms? There are many possibilities, including

• something you ate or drank

• a medication you took

• food poisoning

• early pregnancy

• a stomach disorder

• a viral or bacterial infection

WHEN TO CALL THE DOCTOR

Call 9-1-1 immediately:

- If you're experiencing abdominal pain, blurred vision, muscle weakness, difficulty speaking or swallowing, or muscle paralysis. This could be botulism.
- If with nausea and vomiting you are sweating or dizzy, have very teary eyes or excessive saliva, or experience mental confusion or abdominal pain 30 minutes after eating. This can signal pesticide poisoning or other deadly contamination.
- If you vomit blood or material that resembles coffee grounds

Call your doctor for:

- Bloody or tarry stools
- Symptoms of dehydration
- Swelling or pain in the abdomen or rectum
- Symptoms that recur
- Symptoms that last more than two to three days
- Symptoms with a fever of 101.5°F or higher

- migraine headache
- head injury
- inner ear infection
- stress
- recreational drug use
- binge-purge eating disorders
- visual disturbances
- fear

The bottom line is that nausea and vomiting are not caused by any single factor. And they're not illnesses in themselves. They're symptoms of something else going on with your body.

When to Halt the Heaves

While your first inclination after vomiting is to find some way to stop it from happening again, this emetic rush is really your friend because it often literally gets rid of whatever is ailing you. On occasion, however, nausea and vomiting drag on. While you may be able to cope with ongoing nausea, there are risks to repeated vomiting. If you vomit a lot or for many days, you can become dehydrated quickly. And if vomiting accompanies morning sickness, the nutritional flow to the developing fetus may be impaired.

Because nausea and vomiting are usually just sideshows and not the main event, under most circumstances they can be remedied right in your kitchen without too much fuss or muss. Here are several kitchen-centered ways to put them in their place.

FROM THE CUPBOARD

PEPPERMINT CANDY. Peppermint candy can remedy nausea. Peppermint anesthetizes the stomach, which reduces the gag reflex and stops vomiting. Suck on a piece or two to rid yourself of the symptoms.

POPCORN. Air pop a cup or two and place in a bowl. Skip the butter and salt. Instead, pour enough boiling water over the popcorn to cover it, then let it stand for 15 minutes. Take 1 teaspoon every ten minutes for nausea. Popcorn is a carbohydrate, which is especially needed if you've been vomiting or skipping meals, and the added water is good for dehydration.

SALT. To stop that vomiting, mix together 1 heaping teaspoon salt, 1 heaping teaspoon red pepper, and 1 cup vinegar. Take 1 tablespoon every half hour, as needed.

SODA CRACKERS. Chewing on a few of these can help quell nausea.

VINEGAR. To stop the nausea of morning sickness, stir 1 teaspoon apple cider vinegar into 1 glass water and drink.

FROM THE REFRIGERATOR

CRANBERRY JUICE. Avoiding solid food for a day is sometimes recommended when you're nauseated and vomit-

NAUSEA-FRIENDLY FOODS

Even though you're queasy, you've got to eat something. Isn't that what your mother always told you? Well, she was right. Nausea and vomiting can lead to dehydration and a depletion in vital nutrients, so unless you're fully engaged in a bout of vomiting, here are some foods that might go down easily: rice, cooked cereal, crackers, puddings, low fat milkshakes, fruit salad, cottage cheese. Also, try mixing a little white rice with cottage cheese. It has little visual appeal and its taste is pretty bland, but it digests easily.

ing, but don't give up the fluids. Drink cranberry juice during your fast. It's generally easy on your digestive tract.

LEMON JUICE. Mix together 1 teaspoon honey and 1 teaspoon lemon juice. And this cure comes with a folkish instruction: Dip your finger into the mix and lick it off so that you take it in slowly.

LIME JUICE. For an immediate nausea/vomiting stopper, mix 1 cup water, 10 drops lime juice, and ½ teaspoon sugar. Then add ¼ teaspoon baking soda and drink.

MILK. Don't drink it straight. Instead, try this vintage milk toast recipe for a bland food that's easy to eat when combating nausea and vomiting. Heat 1 cup milk until hot but not boiling. Put it in a bowl. Then take 1 piece of toast, slightly buttered, and crumble it into the milk. Eat slowly.

ONION. Juice an onion to make 1 teaspoon. Mix with 1 teaspoon grated ginger and take for nausea.

FROM THE SPICE RACK

ANISEED. This helps cure nausea and vomiting. Brew aniseed into a tea by putting ¼ teaspoon in ½ cup boiling water. Steep for five minutes. Strain and drink once a day. Or sprinkle some aniseed on mild vegetables such as carrots or pumpkin. If your stomach will tolerate fruits during or just after a bout of nausea or vomiting, try aniseed on baked apples or pears.

CARDAMOM SEEDS. To relieve nausea, chew 1 to 2 cardamom seeds. Another cardamom cure is to mix 2 pinches ground cardamom and ½ teaspoon honey into ½ cup plain yogurt. It will relieve nausea, and it's also a nutritious food to eat when you can't keep anything else down.

CINNAMON. Steep ½ teaspoon cinnamon powder in 1 cup boiling water, strain, and sip for nausea. Do not try this remedy if you're pregnant.

CLOVE. This makes a nice nausea-fighting tea. Brew a cup using 1 teaspoon clove powder in a teacup full of boiling water. Strain out any clove that might be remaining, and drink as needed.

CUMIN. Steep a tea with 1 teaspoon cumin seeds and a pinch of nutmeg to soothe tummy troubles.

FENNEL. Crush 1 tablespoon seeds and steep for ten minutes in 1 cup boiling water. Sweeten to taste with honey. Sip as necessary for nausea.

GINGER. Without a doubt, ginger is the best stomach woe cure of all. Taken in any form, it will relieve nausea. Try ginger tea, gingerbread, or gingersnaps. If you're traveling, take along ginger sticks or crystallized ginger instead of travel sickness pills or patches. Studies show ginger to be more effective than the potion you purchase at the pharmacy. Skip the ginger ales, though, unless they have real ginger content. Much of today's ginger ale is absent its curative ginger.

FASCINATING FACT

Smell can exacerbate nausea and bring on vomiting. If you're feeling a little queasy, stay away from cooking smells, especially fried and spicy foods. Also skip the foods about which you have negative thoughts. Just the thought of those foods really can make you sick.

MINT. Mint tea relieves nausea. Simply steep about 1 tablespoon dry leaves in 1 pint hot water for 30 minutes; strain and drink. Don't toss out those mint leaves when you drink the tea. Instead, eat them. Eating boiled mint leaves can cure nausea, too.

MORE DO'S & DON'TS

• Hit the bed. Rest is the best cure for whatever's causing your nausea or vomiting.

• Skip the booze. It can be hard on the stomach even under the best of circumstances. While you're at it, avoid these gut-wreckers, too: fatty or highly seasoned foods, caffeine, and cigarettes.

• If you must take an over-the-counter remedy, try one with bismuth, such as Pepto-Bismol. It will coat the stomach and relieve discomfort. Skip the fizzy seltzer stuff, though. It contains aspirin, which may be irritating to an already upset stomach.

• After you vomit, rinse the remaining particles out of your mouth with ¼ cup water and ¼ cup vinegar in a 4-ounce glass. The stomach acids in vomit can be harsh on tooth enamel. Just rinse, don't gargle. This freshens your breath, too.

Prostate Problems
PAMPER YOUR PROSTATE

It's a sad fact of growing older for the male species. Most men over the age of 60 (and some in their 50s) develop some symptoms of prostate problems. The three most common disorders are benign prostatic hyperplasia (BPH), a noncancerous enlargement of the prostate; prostatitis, an inflammatory infection; and prostate cancer. BPH is so common that some physicians consider it a normal consequence of aging in males.

The prostate's main role is to produce an essential portion of the seminal fluid that carries sperm. This walnut-shaped gland located just below a man's bladder starts to kick in near puberty and continues to grow and grow. This enlargement doesn't usually cause symptoms until after age 40, and it usually doesn't cause problems until age 60 or later.

An enlarged prostate is problematic because it presses on the urethra, creating difficulties with urination and weakening the bladder. Some of the symptoms of prostate problems include the following:

- difficulty urinating

- frequent urination, especially at night

- difficulty starting urination

- an inability to empty the bladder

- a dribble of urine despite the urgent need to urinate

- a burning sensation when urinating

- uncontrolled dribbling after urination

- pain behind the scrotum

- painful ejaculation

Ignoring prostate problems, as some men are wont to do, isn't a smart idea. Left untreated, prostate problems can get progressively worse, become more painful, and can lead to dangerous complications, including bladder and kidney infections.

Changes in diet can help relieve some prostate discomforts and, in some cases, may reduce the chances of developing prostate cancer. Check out how the kitchen can help your prostate.

FROM THE CUPBOARD

PUMPKIN SEEDS. Pumpkin seeds are used by German doctors to treat difficult urination that accompanies an enlarged prostate that is not cancerous. The seeds contain diuretic properties and plenty of zinc, which helps repair and build the immune system. The tastiest way to enjoy pumpkin seeds is to eat them plain. Remove the shells and don't add salt. You can also try a tea. Crush a handful of fresh seeds and place in the bottom of a 1-pint jar. Fill with boiling water. Let cool to room temperature. Strain and drink a pint of pumpkin seed tea a day.

FROM THE REFRIGERATOR

CORN SILK. The silk from corn has been used by Amish men for generations as a remedy for the symptoms of prostate enlargement. When fresh corn is in season, cut the silk from 6 ears of corn. (Corn silk can be dried for later use, too.) Put in 1 quart water, boil, and simmer for ten minutes. Strain and drink a cup. Drink 3 cups a week.

WHEN TO CALL THE DOCTOR

- If you experience one or more of the symptoms listed on page 168
- For an annual prostate cancer test

FISH. From the deep comes a way to fight prostate cancer and tumor growth. Try to get 2 servings a week of fish high in omega-3 oils (the good oil) such as tuna, mackerel, or salmon.

SOY. Learning to like and use soy foods is an easy and good way to help nip prostate problems in the bud. Soy-based foods contain phytoestrogens, which are thought to help reduce testosterone production, which is believed to aggravate prostate cancer growth. The phytoestrogens are believed to limit the growth of blood capillaries that form around tumors of the prostate.

TOMATOES. Seize that salsa! Pour on the spaghetti sauce! Down that tomato juice! Learn to add more tomatoes to your diet. Studies have shown that as little as 2 servings of tomatoes (including cooked tomatoes) a week can help men reduce their risk of prostate cancer by half. These red orbs are full of lycopene, an antioxidant compound that helps fight cancer.

FASCINATING FACT

Approximately 1 out of every 10 men in the United States develops cancer of the prostate. Despite this alarming statistic, more men die *with* prostate cancer than *from* the cancer. Most pass away due to other ailments such as heart disease and stroke.

WATERMELON SEEDS. The Amish use watermelon tea to flush the system out and help with bladder and prostate problems. Enjoy a slice of watermelon and spit the seeds in a cup. When you have ⅛ cup fresh watermelon seeds, put them in a 1-pint jar and fill with boiling water. Let the tea cool, strain, and drink. Drink 1 pint of tea every day for ten days.

FROM THE SUPPLEMENT SHELF

SAW PALMETTO. The extract of the berries of this plant has been shown to work as well or better than prescription drugs in improving urinary flow rates and reducing the symptoms of BPH, such as urinary hesitancy and weak flow. The extract works by altering certain hormone levels, thus reducing prostate enlargement. Palmetto extracts can be purchased at the health food store. Consult your physician for recommended dosages.

STINGING NETTLE. Stinging nettle has been used in Europe for more than a decade, and studies have shown it to reduce symptoms of prostate problems. Nettle helps by inhibiting binding of testosterone-related proteins to their receptor sites on prostate cell membranes. Take stinging nettle in extract form (as capsules). Check with your physician for the correct dosage.

MORE DO'S AND DON'TS

- Drink 8 glasses of water a day.

- Limit your intake of fatty foods and red meats.

- Schedule an annual prostate exam. Catching problems early is vital.

- Watch your alcohol intake. Studies have shown that beer can raise prolactin levels in the body, which in turn can eventually lead to prostate enlargement.

Sore Throat
RELIEVING RAWNESS

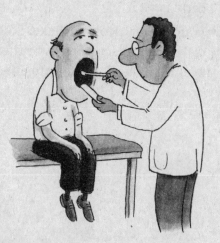

It's scratchy, tender, and swollen, and you dread the simple task of swallowing. But you must swallow, and when you do, you brace yourself for the unavoidable pain. If you've got a sore throat, you're in good company; everybody gets them, and 40 million people trek to the doctor's office for treatment of one every year.

The mechanics of a sore throat are pretty simple. It's an inflammation of the pharynx, which is the tube that extends from the back of the mouth to the esophagus. The following are the leading causes of sore throat:

- Viral infection (colds, flu, etc.). Often accompanied by fever, achy muscles, and runny nose, viral infections can't be cured but their symptoms can be treated. A sore throat from a viral source will generally disappear on its own within several days.

- Bacterial infection, especially from a streptococcal bacteria (strep throat). Symptoms are much like those of a viral infection but may be more severe and long lasting.

Often a bacterial infection is accompanied by headache, stomachache, and swollen glands in the neck. A strep infection is generally treated with antibiotics because permanent heart or kidney damage can result. Culturing the bacteria is the only way a doctor can determine the cause of the sore throat.

While those are the primary reasons for a sore throat, there are others, including

- Smoking
- Acid reflux
- Allergies
- Dry air, especially at night when you may sleep with your mouth open
- Mouth breathing
- Throat abuse: singing, shouting, coughing
- Polyps or cancer
- Infected tonsils
- Food allergy

Whatever the cause, you want a cure when your throat's on fire. In some cases,

WHEN TO CALL THE DOCTOR

- If you have a swollen throat and are having difficulty breathing, call 9-1-1 or seek immediate emergency treatment
- If your sore throat lasts more than four days
- If you suspect a serious infection such as strep
- If you have a fever over 103°F or any fever lasting more than three days
- If you have a skin rash
- If swallowing is very painful
- If sore throat is accompanied by an earache
- If you have achy joints
- If you have blisters or pus in your throat
- If you're spitting up bloody phlegm
- If a sore throat keeps you from normal activities
- For any sore throat in infants, young children, people with weakened immune systems, or older people

LARYNGITIS? SHUSH!

If you've got laryngitis, don't whisper. The whispering movement on your vocal chords is just as bad for you as shouting. To get that voice back, talk quietly or be silent. And moisturize those vocal chords to help them heal. Drink 8 to 10 glasses of water a day, and drink ginger tea and inhale steam.

medical attention is definitely required to cure the underlying infection. But there are soothing remedies to be found in the kitchen that can stand alone or work side-by-side with traditional medicine to stifle that soreness.

FROM THE CUPBOARD

CIDER VINEGAR. This sore throat cure is found in several different remedies. Here are a few of the more popular types of uses:

For sipping: Mix 1 tablespoon each of honey and cider vinegar in 1 cup warm water.

For gargling: You'll need 1 teaspoon salt, ½ cup cider vinegar, and 1 cup warm water. Dissolve the salt in the vinegar, then mix in the water. Gargle every 15 minutes as necessary.

For soaking: Soak cheesecloth or gauze in ⅔ cup warm water with 2 tablespoons cider vinegar. Wring out and apply to the throat, covering it with dry gauze to keep it in place. Wear it all night.

HORSERADISH. Try this Russian sore throat cure. Combine 1 tablespoon pure horseradish or horseradish root with 1 teaspoon honey and 1 teaspoon ground cloves. Mix in a glass of warm water and drink slowly.

LEMON JUICE. Mix 1 tablespoon each of honey and lemon juice in 1 cup warm water. Sip this mixture.

LIME JUICE. Combine 1 spoonful with a spoonful of honey and take as often as needed for a sore throat.

SALT. Yes, when your mother told you to gargle with salt water, she knew what she was talking about. It cuts phlegm and reduces inflammation. Dissolve ½ teaspoon salt in ½ cup warm water and gargle gently every three to four hours.

FROM THE FREEZER

JUICE BAR. This is cold and soothing to a hot throat. Don't suck, though. Sucking may irritate the throat even more. Simply let small pieces melt in your mouth.

FROM THE REFRIGERATOR

BEETS. Make a poultice by grating 2 to 3 tablespoons red beets and covering them with 2 cups boiling water. Soak a clean towel in the warm solution, wring it out, and apply to the throat. Remove when cold and reapply as often as

Recipe Box

AMISH ONION & HONEY SORE THROAT SOOTHER

6 white onions, finely chopped
1 cup honey
juice of 1 fresh lemon
2 tablespoons olive oil

Sauté onions in olive oil until transparent, stirring often. Stir in the honey (use brown sugar if recipe is for children under age 2). Add lemon juice. Continue to cook over low heat until mixture thickens. Remove, pour in glass jar. Take 1 tablespoon as often as needed. Store in refrigerator.

necessary. Beets will stain the cloth (and your skin) so use a towel that you don't mind turning reddish purple.

ONIONS. This tear-promoting veggie contains allicin, which can kill the bacteria that causes strep. Eat them raw or sautéd. And check the Recipe Box, page 175, for an Amish sore throat soother.

RASPBERRIES. These can make a great gargle (see Recipe Box below). If you also have a fever, the gargle can be used as a fever-reducing drink, too. Do not drink any liquid you have used as a gargle.

FROM THE SINK

WATER. Gargle with 4 parts water to 1 part three-percent hydrogen peroxide two to three times a day. Also, sip plain water throughout the day to prevent your throat from becoming dry.

FROM THE SPICE RACK

CINNAMON. Mix 2 parts cinnamon, 2 parts ginger, and 3 parts licorice powder. Steep 1 teaspoon of this mixture in

RASPBERRY GARGLE

2 cups ripe red raspberries
2½ cups white wine vinegar
1 cup sugar

Place berries in a bowl and cover with the vinegar. Cover, and leave in a cool place three days. Place the mixture in a saucepan, add sugar, and bring to a gentle boil. Simmer 15 minutes, remove from heat, and cool. Strain through a sieve, pressing down the berries to retrieve as much juice as possible. Store in a bottle, refrigerate, and use as needed.

1 cup boiling water for ten minutes, then drink as a sore throat cure three times a day. **GARLIC.** This Amish remedy can treat or prevent sore throats. Peel a fresh clove, slice it in half, and place 1 piece in each cheek. Suck on the garlic like a cough drop. Occasionally, crush your teeth against the garlic, not to bite it in half but to release its allicin, a chemical that can kill the bacteria that causes strep.

> ### GIVE IT SOME ZINC
> Zinc lozenges may relieve a sore throat. Suck on 1 lozenge every two hours. And because high doses of vitamin C are often recommended in treating a sore throat (it doesn't cure the throat problem but it does boost the immune system), ask your pharmacist about vitamin C lozenges.

MARJORAM. Make a soothing tea with a spoonful of marjoram steeped in a cup of boiling water for ten minutes. Strain, then sweeten to taste with honey.

PEPPERMINT OIL. Add 2 drops each of peppermint and eucalyptus oils to 2 teaspoons olive oil, and massage on the throat and upper chest for a nice, relaxing throat-soother.

SAGE. This curative herb is a great sore throat gargle. Mix 1 teaspoon in 1 cup boiling water. Steep for ten minutes, then strain. Add 1 teaspoon each cider vinegar and honey, then gargle four times a day.

TURMERIC. Try this gargle to calm a cranky throat. Mix together 1 cup hot water, ½ teaspoon turmeric, and ½ teaspoon salt. Gargle with the mixture twice a day. If you're not good with the gargle, mix ½ teaspoon turmeric in 1 cup hot milk and drink. Turmeric stains clothing, so be careful when mixing and gargling.

FROM THE STOVE

STEAM. With or without herbs, inhaling steam can relieve the discomfort of a sore throat. Heat a pot full of water, remove from heat, make a tent with a towel, and place your face over the steam. (Make sure your head is high enough that the steam can't burn your face.) Then inhale. Adding 1 to 2 drops eucalyptus oil can be soothing.

MORE DO'S & DON'TS

• Drink plenty of fluids, especially fruit juices.

• Nix the colas and scratchy foods, such as chips and pretzels. They'll irritate an already irritated throat.

• Rest. This will allow your body to build up the defenses to fight off whatever's causing your sore throat.

Stress
PUTTING PRESSURE IN ITS PLACE

Stress. We all know what that's about, don't we? The traffic in your life is jamming up. Everything is fast-paced, high-pressured, loaded with responsibility. Some people thrive on that roller-coaster rhythm, but others don't, and the stress in their lives begins to take a toll, physically and mentally. The stress alters body chemistry and affect immunity. You know that heart attack someone suffered because he was "all stressed out"? Stress changed his body chemistry; it contributed to a hormonal imbalance that increased the rate at which plaque was hardening his arteries, and it altered the production and distribution of his body fat. The result of his stress: heart attack. And that psoriasis she suffers? Stress caused her nerve cells to produce a chemical that stopped immune cells from fighting the red, itchy skin disease she's plagued with.

So, how's your stress level? If you answer yes to the following questions, then read on. You may benefit from some of the stress cures from the kitchen.

WHEN TO SEE THE DOCTOR

- When you're experiencing symptoms. Stress symptoms mimic the symptoms of other serious illness, including thyroid disease, therefore it's vital that your doctor determine the cause of your problem.
- When stress interferes with normal daily activity, and home treatments do not work. There are medications available that can remedy symptoms.
- When stress causes *any* kind of chest pain, even mild pain

Stress on the job:

1. Are you overworked, underappreciated, or both?
2. Does it take everything you've got, physically, mentally, or both, just to make it from 9 to 5?

Stress at home:

1. Do you have enough time for the fun things?
2. Do people expect more from you than you want to give?
3. Are there some important relationships that should be better?
4. Are there some changes you'd really like to make in yourself?

If you find yourself muttering "yes" to half of these, you're stressed. To what degree depends on your ability to cope with stress. But if you need a little stress relief, you'll find it in the remedies that follow.

FROM THE CUPBOARD

BAKING SODA. A soothing bath in baking soda and ginger can relieve stress. Add ⅓ cup ginger and ⅓ cup baking soda to a tub of hot water and enjoy the soak.

OATS. Besides fighting off high cholesterol, oats produce a calming effect that fights off stress. Use them in bread

EASY OATCAKES

6 ounces regular oatmeal
½ teaspoon salt
½ ounce butter, softened
Additional oatmeal

Mix oatmeal and salt in bowl. Add butter and 5 ounces boiling water, and mix into a sticky dough. Let it stand for five minutes to allow oatmeal to expand. Then, sprinkle flat surface with a few tablespoons of oatmeal, turn dough out onto it, and knead lightly. Roll dough out as thinly as possible, sprinkling with more oatmeal to prevent sticking, then cut into circles, squares, or desired shapes. Bake at 325°F for 15 to 20 minutes until dry and crisp but not browned. Use as you would a cracker.

recipes and desserts or for thickening in soups. Or just eat a bowl of oatmeal! See Recipe Box, above, for a healthy oatcake.

PASTA. When you're faced with eating a late-night meal, choose pasta. It causes a rise in the brain chemical called serotonin, which has a calming effect on the body. Rice produces the same effect.

SALT. Try this muscle-soothing bath to wash that stress away. Mix ½ cup salt, 1 cup Epsom salts, and 2 cups baking soda. Add ½ cup of the mix to your bathwater. Store the dry mix in a covered container, away from moisture.

SESAME OIL. For a nice relaxation technique, warm a few ounces and rub it all over your body, from head to toe. Sunflower and corn oil work well, too. After your massage, take a long, hot soak in the tub.

WHOLE-WHEAT BREAD. It's high in the B vitamins, which sustain the nervous system. Other B-rich foods include whole-wheat pita bread, whole-grain cereal, pasta, and brown rice. For a good stress-fighting diet, about 60 percent of your daily calories should come from these starchy foods, divided among your meals.

FROM THE DRAWER

BALLOON. Red, blue, purple...it's your choice. To make a stress ball, fill a small balloon with baking soda, tie off the opening, and simply squeeze your stress away.

FROM THE REFRIGERATOR

CELERY. The phytonutrients called phthalides found in celery have a widely recognized sedative effect, so eat your celery whole or chopped into a salad.

CHERRIES. They soothe the nervous system and relieve stress. Eat them fresh or any way you like them.

LETTUCE. This stress-reducing veggie has a sedative effect. A small amount of lactucarium, a natural sedative, is found in the white, milky juice that oozes from the lettuce when the stalk is snapped.

FROM THE SPICE RACK

CARDAMOM SEEDS. These are said to freshen the breath, speed the digestion, and cheer the heart. But they also bust the stress. To make a tea, cover 2 to 3 pods with boiling water and steep for ten minutes. Cardamom pods can be added to a regular pot of tea, too, in order to derive the calming effect. Also, crush the pods and add to rice or lentils before cooking, or use in a vegetable stir-fry. If you like the taste, cardamom seeds are a good addition to cakes and biscuits. Instead of pods, you can use 1 teaspoon powdered cardamom, which is available in the spice section of the grocery store.

PEPPERMINT. Drink a cup of peppermint tea before bed to relieve tension and help you sleep. Chamomile, catnip, or vervain works well, too. Place 1 teaspoon of the dried leaf in a cup of boiling water. Sweeten with honey and sip before bed. To reap the fullest benefits, sipping this sooth-ing tea should be the last thing you do before you tuck yourself in for the night. And during the day, if you don't have time for a cup of tea, try a peppermint. Read the label for a good variety, though. One with peppermint, sugar, and little else is best. The more extra ingredients that go into the candy, the less the relaxing benefit.

TARRAGON. A tarragon tea calms the nervous system. Add ½ teaspoon dried tarragon to 1 cup boiling water. Or use it fresh, snipped into salads or vegetables. It's a good season-ing for creamy soups, too, or added to a salad dressing of balsamic vinegar with a dash of honey.

MORE DO'S & DON'TS

• Seek support. It's easier to cope when someone is there to hold your hand.

• Choose control. You can't control everything in your life, but a little control can go a long way in fighting stress. Make a list of things you can control and things you can't control. When you see it in print, you'll be surprised how much of your life is already under your control. That, in itself, should relieve some stress.

Make 'em Laugh

Can you laugh stress away? Maybe not completely, but a hearty chuckle helps. In addition to making you feel better, laughing has other benefits.

- Laughing uses 15 facial muscles, and it's a great muscle toner.
- When you're laughing, your pulse and breathing speed up. This increases the amount of oxygen carried in the blood, giving your vital organs a vital boost in energy.
- After you laugh, there's a period of muscular relaxation that can bring physical relief to those with arthritis or nerve pain.
- For asthmatics and others who suffer lung problems, laughing increases air exchange in the lungs, increasing oxygen circulation and clearing out mucus plugs.
- Laughing exercises the heart muscle.
- The immune system is boosted by the increased circulation that comes from laughing. This helps the body fight infection and reduces the risk of blood clots.

- **Find your purpose.** Having a purpose can relieve stress, and if nothing special comes to mind, create a purpose. Volunteer at a homeless shelter, make new friends at a nursing home. When you involve yourself in something other than your stress, your stress will actually decrease.

- **Exercise.** The endorphins released in 20 minutes of aerobic exercise have a feel-good effect that reduces stress.

- **Nix the artificial stimulants.** Caffeine, nicotine, alcohol—it may seem like they relieve stress, but the effect is only temporary. In the long run, they can make you anxious and cause you more health problems.

- **Relax.** Take some deep breaths. Give your stressed-out muscles a break by soaking in a nice warm tub. Or listen to relaxing music, read a book, meditate, or pray.

Ulcers
HEALING THE HOLE

It's only in the last decade that scientific evidence conclusively proved that ulcers are most often caused by a bacterial infection, not by the Type-A, pressure-cooker personality that was the subject of countless jokes. Misconceptions and myths die hard, though, so there are some people who haven't gotten the word yet and still believe that the demanding boss or the overachiever are more likely to work themselves into an ulcer. While these personality characteristics may aggravate an existing ulcer (not to mention the people they associate with), they don't cause one.

There's a Hole in the Bucket

An ulcer is a sore or hole in the protective mucosal lining of the gastrointestinal tract. Ulcers appear in the area of the stomach or the duodenum, the upper part of the small intestine, where caustic digestive juices, pepsin, and hydrochloric acid are present. Today we know that the majority of ulcers are the result of an infection with a bacteria called *Helicobacter pylori (H. pylori)*. This bacteria makes the stomach and small intestine more susceptible to the erosive effects of the digestive juices. The bacteria may also cause the stomach to produce more acid.

There are some lifestyle factors that can contribute to the development of an ulcer. These include alcohol consumption, eating and drinking foods that contain caffeine, significant physical (not emotional) stress such as severe burns and major surgery, and excessive use of certain over-the-counter pain medications such as aspirin or ibuprofen. Studies have shown that smoking also tends to increase the chances of developing an ulcer, slows the healing of existing ulcers, and makes a recurrence more likely. Family history of ulcers also seems to play a role in susceptibility.

Who Gets Ulcers?

If Type-A folks don't automatically get ulcers, then who does? The cause lies less in personality and more in stomach makeup. Researchers believe some people just produce more stomach acid than others. If stomach acid production isn't the problem, then a weak stomach may be. The stomach lining in certain individuals may be less able to withstand the onslaught of gastric acids. Lifestyle factors (see above) can also weaken the stomach's lining.

Signs and Symptoms

You're probably familiar with the most typical symptom of a brewing ulcer: a burning or gnawing pain between the breastbone and navel. This pain is more common between meals (it improves with eating but returns a few hours later) and in the middle of the night or toward dawn.

Less typical symptoms include nausea or vomiting, weight loss and loss of appetite, and frequent burping or bloating.

If you have an ulcer or suspect you may have one, you should be under the care of a physician. But between visits to the doctor, there are ways to care for your digestive tract.

FROM THE COUNTER

BANANAS. These fruits contain an antibacterial substance that may inhibit the growth of ulcer-causing *H. pylori*. And studies show that animals fed bananas have a thicker stomach wall and greater mucus production in the stomach, which helps build a better barrier between digestive acids and the lining of the stomach. Eating plantains is also helpful.

GARLIC. Garlic's antibacterial properties include fighting *H. pylori*. Take two small crushed cloves a day.

FROM THE REFRIGERATOR

CABBAGE. Researchers have found that ulcer patients who drink 1 quart of raw cabbage juice a day can often heal their ulcers in five days. If chugging a quart of cabbage juice turns your stomach inside out, researchers also found that those who eat plain cabbage have quicker healing times as well. Time for some coleslaw!

Overdoing the Antacids

The medicine cabinet holds what many think is a cure-all for ulcers: antacids. When taken as directed, antacids are your stomach's ally and can relieve the discomfort of an ulcer attack. However, like all medications, antacids come with a dark side. Here's what you need to know to use antacids appropriately:

- Never self-medicate with antacids. Use them as directed by a physician.
- Aluminum-based antacids can cause constipation and may also interfere with absorption of phosphorus from the diet, resulting in muscle and bone weakness and bone loss over a long period.
- Magnesium-based antacids can cause diarrhea.
- Consistent use of antacids may mask the symptoms of more serious disorders.

PLUMS. Red- and purple-colored foods inhibit the growth of *H. pylori*. Like plums, berries too can help you fight the good fight.

From the Spice Rack

CAYENNE PEPPER. Used moderately, a little cayenne pepper can go a long way in helping ulcers. The pepper stimulates blood flow to bring nutrients to the stomach. To make a cup of peppered tea, mix ¼ teaspoon cayenne pepper in 1 cup hot water. Drink a cup a day. A dash of cayenne pepper can also be added to soups, meats, and other savory dishes.

LICORICE. Several modern studies have demonstrated the ulcer-healing abilities of licorice. Licorice does its part not by reducing stomach acid but rather by reducing the ability of stomach acid to damage stomach lining. Properties in licorice encourage digestive mucosal tissues to protect themselves from acid. Licorice can be used in encapsulated form, but for a quick cup of licorice tea, cut 1 ounce licorice root into slices and cover with 1 quart boiling water. Steep, cool, and strain. (If licorice root is unavailable, cut 1 ounce real licorice sticks into slices.) You can also try licorice candy if it's made with real licorice (the label will say licorice mass) and not just flavored with anise. Don't eat more than 1 ounce per day.

MORE DO'S AND DON'TS

- Be like a bunny and nibble throughout the day. The key to keeping gastric juices from attacking the digestive tract lining is to keep them busy with food. Snacking on healthy treats, such as carrot sticks and whole-wheat crackers, should do the trick. Also, consider becoming a six-small-meals-a-day type person rather than a three-meals-a-day type.

- Don't smoke. Smokers have double the risk of developing ulcers. If that's not bad enough, ulcers heal more slowly in smokers, and their relapse rate is higher than normal.

- Limit alcohol intake. The question of alcohol's impact on ulcer formation remains unanswered, but many medical experts believe individuals who drink heavily are at higher risk for ulcer development compared to light drinkers or abstainers.

- Control your stress. All that frustration and anxiety you carry around can aggravate ulcers or make the conditions ripe for one to appear. Work on ways to effectively control (and eliminate) stress. Take a stress management course, learn to meditate, do yoga, or exercise regularly! Do whatever it takes to let go of stress.

Index